BEING SOUL CONFIDENT

YOUR PRACTICAL GUIDE TO CONFIDENT
ALIGNMENT WITH SOUL IN LIFE AND BUSINESS
THROUGH SOUL SIGNATURES

NICOLA TONSAGER

CONTENTS

DEDICATION

For everyone who believes that leading with soul is leading from your deepest evolving truth - love.

For Dad, Grandpa, Darcy and Flynn - you taught me that my capacity for grief was matched only by my capacity for love; our deepest teacher and our most divine essence - thank you xx

PREFACE

You're the journey. You are what life is all about, unfolding fully into all of your potential, into all that is possible. You do that through becoming confident within yourself, confident through soul.

When you move into that deeper wisdom of who you are, it empowers everything within life. You gain confidence, trust and reassurance in your capabilities, abilities, potential and opportunities. You make courageous choices; changes to your life and business so that you can live life your way. You align your life and business with your non-negotiable values, creating a greater sense of freedom, joy and purpose.

You trust your path, life, and yourself within life. Being soul-led brings you to the heart of your journey; you are being soul confident.

INTRODUCTION

Picture a young woman. It is 5pm and she is leaving work with a smile and wave. As soon as she is out into the cold, rainy London evening, her demeanour changes and the smile fades as if it never was.

Depression's grey, murky cloak tightens its grip on her; any lightness that she was pretending was there vanishes and whomever she was or might have been, is smothered from sight once more.

Her footsteps become slower, it's hard to stay upright as the weight of grey bears down and makes it difficult to function.

She is holding herself so tightly, she is literally allowing her mind to bind her, to hold her in just to get through the day. She goes to work, she does her job to earn what she needs to pay the bills and the effort it takes to do that just wipes her out. It leaves her dead inside.

She tries to push against it but when she does, the cloak just wraps itself even tighter around her. She's too scared to push again because she knows she can't take any more of the monster bearing down. It's already overshadowing everything about her and her life, oppressing, smothering, almost asphyxiating the very breath of life out of her. She simply hasn't got any more to give.

One cold, October evening, she breaks. She just collapses in on herself. The pressure of life, the pressure of just trying to exist within life with this dank, dark greyness suffocating her is just too much.

Like a volcano, everything erupts. She can't stop crying. She has panic attacks and can't breathe. Her chest feels tight, like her lungs are on fire, pressing in on her, crushing her. She is being crushed alive inside and, on some level, she knows she won't get through it. She has no reserves of energy; her physical vitality is non-existent. There is nothing left.

That October evening changes her life.

She didn't want to die, yet she is afraid that is where she is heading.

Sitting on the floor of her living room, hunched over, rocking back and forth, she cries until her eyes are raw, repeating "I can't do this, I can't do this anymore. Please, somebody, just help me."

She's praying but she isn't really hoping and then, suddenly, she feels something. Something moves within her. Everything goes quiet, she stops rocking, stops crying. She gasps, and that moment of breath allows an expansion within her.

She's never felt anything like this before; she doesn't know what it is but suddenly, she just knows she will be ok.

A warmth rises from the pit of her stomach, rising all the way through her and in that moment, it takes everything else away. It is almost like the glow on a gorgeous summer evening when that ripple of energy from the sun reaches out and soothes you. You step out into it and instantly feel lifted and restored.

As quickly as it rises, it goes. She feels almost empty, almost numb and yet she is full. There is a lightness in her being that she has not experienced for so many years. She doesn't realise at the time what has occurred; she just knows something has and that life and hope, somehow, are returning.

It takes her two more years to fully move through depression. To feel a vitality and a spark more days than not. It takes her two more years to want to fully meet life; to want to embrace it; to greet the morning with a true smile and with joy, knowing there is opportunity.

During that time, she dives into energy; learning and exploring so she can make sense of the experience she's had. The only thing of which she is certain from that October evening is that something rose from within her; something inside her had answered that prayer.

Sitting in meditation on a training course, she has the same experience. And suddenly she knows.

It is soul.

Soul had risen directly to meet her in that moment two years before. It had risen to accept her, to hold her and to see her. Soul rose to give her the courage and hope she felt she no longer had on her own.

That moment on an October evening in 1995 changed my life. My experience with soul saved my life and it led me on a journey to know more and to understand what I had experienced.

That journey led me to Soul Signatures and it led me to you. If you are here, know that soul is directly asking to meet you here. Right now. It is asking you to be curious, to be open and to explore what might be possible.

As you journey through these pages, trust what you feel to be true. The language of soul is not written in black and white but through feeling and instinctive knowing. There are no hard edges within soul, no right or wrong, no desire for perfection, and no judgement or blame. There is simply a desire to support and encourage you. A desire to know you more fully and for you to also know yourself and all of your potential.

Soul is an expansive energy which seeks to meet you where you are and enable the truest expression of everything that you are and everything that you do.

It wants you to lead with it so that you are leading from your most powerful truth. Whether in life or in business, it knows the impact and the opportunity that is possible when you commit to your truth; when you feel confident to lead from, and with, soul.

If you're ready, I invite you to commit to that truth right now by leaning into these pages and being soul confident.

Much love, Nicola x

PART I

LEADING WITH SOUL

1

WHY LEAD WITH SOUL?

LEADING with soul has never been more important. Leading your business from soul is essential if you want to create an impact in a way which truly matters - in a way which supports, enables and empowers both you and those you serve, and, lets you feel rock-solid confidence as you lead from that power of soul.

We live in a world which appears to be moving ever faster, demanding more, and in more ways. A world where it is easy to get caught up in life's whirr.

Where burn out is considered to be almost normal, and where it is increasingly easy to lose your sense of self - both within life and within your business - and what truly matters to you and why.

Feeling lost, confused and demotivated, life becomes hard and business even harder. You constantly question what you are doing and why, whether you are on the right path (or any path) when all you really desire is clarity and flow.

You procrastinate over the smallest of decisions, going around and around with seemingly little progress or, if there is, it is progress without the sense of fulfilment you need, without the sense of purpose which supports and authorises you.

The antidote is not to try and change the world, but to reconsider how you can place yourself back at the heart of the journey.

Your journey.

Leading with soul puts you directly at the heart of your journey; it puts your business in alignment with soul - a naturally expansive and opportune energy, which creates possibility and opens potential.

It supports a deeper connection with who you are and understanding what that actually means within all areas of life. It enables clarity about what matters to you and why, supporting your confidence and the conviction to rock that within your life and your business *and* to do it your way.

Yet, what is soul? How do you quantify it? Can you understand it and actively work with it? Isn't it just another 'fad'? How can it lend itself to your business? How can you have confidence in it?

How can something which appears so intangible be made practical, real and relatable, and inspire your confidence? That is what this book is all about. Making soul practical, relatable and so easy to understand and work with that it makes absolutely no sense not to do just that.

Soul Signatures are the most comprehensive way to understand the specific qualities of soul which are present in your life and business, in a way which is clear and just makes sense.

You will be able to see the qualities of soul through your life, through your business, realising how they have supported and enabled you. You will be able to recognise the challenges and growth they have brought and you will be able to understand what they are asking of you as you move forward.

You'll trust that you are guided and supported by a presence that is directly part of who you are and you will know that if you lean in and work with that energy, life will expand, your business will flourish and potential, purpose and opportunity will be met.

When you understand the soul qualities behind your business, and the soul energy leading your life, so much makes sense; *this* is what lends confidence and reassurance, enabling you to be soul confident in all that you do.

It's always been my passion to make energy work practical. To use it, we need to understand it and be able to relate to it. Soul is no different. If we can't relate it to life in a way which works, it remains simply a concept and there is no point in that.

I have worked with energy and holistic practices for over twenty-five years, teaching to practitioner level and mentoring students and clients in their spiritual development. Supporting their individuality has always been at the heart of my work because it is how *you* do what you do that makes the difference.

Looking outside of yourself for the answers is something everyone does, yet the power and presence you need comes from within.

Soul Signatures are the key to stepping into that innate power fully, to being your own light, your own hero and to leading your life and your business your way.

Their aim, and the aim of this book, is quite simple: to give you permission to be you, fully. As you recognise their qualities and lean into those, you will stand more confidently in your authentic authority.

Being Soul Confident.

2

HOW TO USE THIS BOOK

BEING Soul Confident is designed to be a practical guide to enabling just that, through aligning to and working with your Soul Signatures. In 'aligning' I mean specifically enabling the energy of who you are - mind, body, spirit - to be in line and harmonised with the energy of your Soul Signatures.

In Part One, I'll introduce what Soul Signatures are, and how they form your Soul Signatures Profile. I'll be detailing different aspects within each Signature, essentially different lenses which enable understanding within different aspects of life and at different levels so that when you move onto Part Two, you are not just reading information about the Signatures, you are directly relating to them as part of you.

I'll also walk you through how to identify your key Soul Signatures (that is kind of important!).

Part Two is all about the Signatures themselves. You can either read through each one to get an overall sense of them or you can read the ones which relate directly to your profile - this is *my* suggestion as it will support feeling into the energy and it will help to validate your awareness of the Signature within life or business rather than creating information overload by reading all eleven at once!

Self-reflection is your most powerful enabler in understanding and aligning with soul, so have a pen and paper to hand when you are working through Part Two to note down immediate resonances or those things which trigger or create an unexpected response; these can be significant catalysts, so use them.

I've detailed some case studies in Part Three so that you can see how the Signatures coalesce as a whole. It is all well and good having different parts of the puzzle and understanding them in their individuality, and that is important as it will inform you, but you will feel more supported, more guided and more able to align and trust that guidance when you see your profile as a whole. So much will make sense!

Finally, in Part Four, I've encouraged you with some processes to actively, and consciously work with the Signatures so that you can move into their qualities, work with the activations and really lead with soul, being confident in doing that and trusting that you *can* lean into it and let its guidance support you more deeply. There are both practical and energetic practices. Whilst we need to enable soul in a practical way, it *is* primarily energetic and it would be remiss of me not to share ways that you can deepen your connection from an energetic perspective; these will also contribute to more awareness of the subtleties of your own energy.

Whilst soul is present anyway and it will support you irrespective of any conscious work you do, ultimately it wants to share its energy and express that through you. When you consciously lean into soul, when you allow it greater presence through you, it is able to expand and empower a greater essence and a greater level of guidance and direction for you. So, do the work. Look at where you already lean in and celebrate that, but work to support those areas where more is asked.

You have this one beautiful, fragile, exciting, brilliant life that works for you most wonderfully when you work on yourself. Do the work.

Shall we start?

3

WHAT ARE SOUL SIGNATURES?

Soul Signatures are dynamic points of light within the energy matrix of soul.

Imagine soul as a 3-D image oscillating within you. As it does, certain points within it are triggered in response to circumstances, a subconscious need, or as part of your life path. As these points of light trigger, they create situations or experiences which bring certain qualities or traits to the fore so that you can master or embody them, thereby reaping their benefit or gift.

Soul Signatures are a channelled representation of the energy of soul which has been given in order to enable a more direct connection, understanding and awareness of it.

The Signatures connect directly to the expansion, need and expression of your soul and they follow eleven stages of soul expansion that you move through, numerous times and on varying levels, as you journey through life.

They are, by their nature, energetic because soul is an energy, as are we.

Each of the eleven Soul Signatures has specific, relatable qualities that it activates and, once you know what these are, you will be able to see them directly at play in your life and business. Our focus will be on these qualities because they are the *tangible measures* that you can use to align with soul. Tangibility enables confidence and I want you to be confident in trusting and aligning with soul and to do the work aligned through the Soul Signatures.

You will be able to recognise where the Signatures have stretched you and where they have supported you. You will be able to understand why particular patterns or behaviour reoccur, so you'll be able to identify how to change, challenge or mitigate that moving forward. You'll see where you need to lean in further to enable growth or authority, or where you need to surrender to acceptance and greater awareness.

We'll be looking at each of the eleven Soul Signatures in depth, reviewing their qualities and understanding what that means from a business and a personal perspective. You are the most significant influence in your business and therefore, your personal Soul Signatures impact and influence what you bring to your business.

We will be:

- Identifying your four key Soul Signatures so that you can understand the natural qualities of soul that are supporting and guiding you and your business;
- Discovering the specific qualities and traits that your Soul Signatures activate, what growth they support and how they challenge;
- Explaining how to work with them to make the most of their support and guidance; and
- Showing you how to identify your annual Soul Signatures so you can lead your year with confidence as you lean into the natural energy it brings.

4

WHAT IS SOUL?

THE OXFORD ENGLISH Dictionary describes soul as "the spiritual or immaterial part of a human being or animal, regarded as immortal."

Soul is energy. As such, we cannot see it. We cannot touch it because it resides within us yet we *can* experience it.

The experience of soul is always strongest in the moment. We can remember it but the truth of the experience is always felt most deeply in the moment of the experience itself.

Soul is an aspect of the divine (you may call it the Creator, God, the Spirit or the Universe) incarnated within us. We cannot hold the entirety of the divine within us, therefore, soul is a 'drop' of the divine, encapsulated and held directly within the human body during its lifetime.

It resides in our Hara, which is located below our belly button, toward the centre of our abdomen.

Soul has a distinct energy. It is not simply a part which makes up our whole but rather our divine aspect, held separately from but which also forms our whole, and it is here to explore and experience life through us, which is why it encourages us to stretch beyond what we think we are capable of.

Its' desire to experience and express itself through you leads directly to why connecting with soul, allowing it and being soul-led is so important.

When you consciously choose to build a more direct relationship with your soul, as you will through aligning to Soul Signatures, you are tapping into a wealth of universal, divine wisdom which resides within you and which knows exactly what is right for you, at any given moment, and which also may make no logical, rational sense at times!

Your potential and possibilities are not rational. They are things you seek *beyond* your current experience; an instinctive call which you know you are capable of answering, even if you are not sure why you know that.

A call that soul is making.

You have already had numerous intuitive (gut) feelings which have steered you into opportunity and away from obstacles, which have opened doorways you hadn't expected and which have moved you out of danger. Intuition is the way our energy receives the voice of soul in a way that we can learn to interpret and understand. I want to show you how to move beyond that; how to move into a direct and active relationship with soul which you cannot doubt because of the evidence it is presenting to you through your Soul Signatures.

As you identify, recognise and experience those qualities and activations which soul is enabling with and for you, as part of life and within your business as part of its evolution, you won't simply be interpreting the energy or voice of soul - you will be living it. You will be partnering with it, for the greatest growth at any given moment. You will be opening the door to a potential you didn't even realise was available for you because you will be *choosing to consciously collaborate* with the divine energy that is part of who you are, rather than it simply being a more passive partner in your journey.

You will be leading with soul.

As you do, you'll be Being Soul Confident.

5

YOUR SOUL SIGNATURES PROFILE

As I INTRODUCED PREVIOUSLY, there are eleven Soul Signatures. You have *all* of them as part of your soul energy and they form a journey of soul unfoldment, with each bringing their gift of learning and opportunity for growth.

They will activate within you many times, at varying levels, during your lifetime, and that of your business. During times of change and challenge, as you step up and dig deeper, you uncover different levels of being; as you unfold different strengths and awareness, you up-level, meeting your expanded self and moving through limitations of the mind, energy and knowledge to step into a different stage within yourself, within life and within your business. With each process of growth and at each new stage of life development, Signatures activate at the appropriate level to support your forward movement with greater confidence, ease and courage.

As you start to become familiar with the Soul Signatures, you'll be able to work with them, and indeed *choose* to activate specific Signatures, to more fully enable you to lead your life and your business with soul and to not only meet but embrace the process of life at any given time.

Out of the eleven Signatures, some are more aligned with you and your path than others. These are more active in their energy and presence within your life, or the life of your business. In a similar way to an astrology chart, which pinpoints specific planetary aspects at the time of your birth that lend their influence in a particular way as you move through life, so the Soul Signatures which form your Soul Signatures Profile, are more influential and impactful.

In this chapter, we'll look at the four Signatures which make up your soul profile, both personally and for your business. But first, because you are the journey, and soul experiences and enables its journey through you, let's have a look at the Soul Signatures journey:

Initiation starts the journey, opening new doors and encouraging curiosity about life and about yourself. As the journey deepens, ***Resonance*** enables greater belief, deeper self-trust and an awareness that you are more than you know. This leads to a ***Commitment*** to your deeper truth. Standing in your power and allowing the essence of who you are to come forth more fully, you ***Anchor*** in reinvention which enables a deeper opening of soul. The ***Feminine*** attributes of empowered intuition start leading, supported by the framework and discipline of the **Masculine** energy which creates the structure within which your soul finds its vision. With **Emergence**, that vision becomes known, establishing new potential. You realise what is possible, a connection with the divinity you are so much a part of, and a **Surrender** to your purpose, to all that you are, is accepted. With this newfound awareness, **Transformation** enables an expansion of energy and internal freedom, leading to the fullest **Integration** of self through the realisations and learnings that your journey has encompassed as you evolve into **Devotion**, gaining mastery over this aspect of life and leading in alignment with soul.

6

THE KEY SIGNATURE ACTIVATIONS WHICH FORM YOUR SOUL SIGNATURES PROFILE

Foundation Signature Activation

THIS IS the energy *supporting you,* or your business, and which always remains constant. It is the Soul Signature which provides the platform for the voice that soul wishes to enable through you and for you.

This Signature always brings you back to who you are and it can be used to realign your energy and focus; to realign the focus of your business with key values to ensure you are building on appropriate foundations.

It anchors you and it provides solid, grounded roots from which to extend upwards. You are asked to master the qualities and activations of your foundational Soul Signature as you move through life, as your business evolves and as life and experience develop.

Leading Signature Activation

This Soul Signature is lighting the way. It is the aim, the ambition and the direction of travel. It holds the potential, which is possible if you can *meet the ask* of the Soul Signatures energy that is represented.

Unlike the foundation activation, its qualities are an 'ask' rather than a given. If you can meet the ask, potential unfolds in a more aligned way.

Growth meets expansion and expansion offers opportunity.

The leading activation provides a destination to journey toward. As you embark on that journey, there may be changes within life or business which alter your direction. There may be opportunities which influence how you navigate forward and these are the Inner and External Influences.

Inner Influence

From a personal perspective, the inner influence is a focus which you choose to enable, albeit sometimes subconsciously. You can choose to align more fully with an inner influence and you can even change it to something which enables more growth or alignment.

From a business perspective, it is a fixed inner influence - the personal influence you bring which directly impacts your business.

External Influence

On a personal level, the external influence relates to changes which have occurred in relation to your leading activation. Depending what these are, they can influence significantly or not make much impact at all. Again, as with your personal inner influence, you can choose to activate different Signatures which you feel may align more and I'll be talking about this when we look at how to identify your Soul Signatures.

From a business perspective, the external influence can stem from your personal leading activation or a variation of your business's leading activation.

The Signatures enable specific qualities which they ask you to align with and embody; their activations ask you to master them. Soul is never static; it is always moving, evolving and expanding. Therefore, as you identify your Signatures, I invite you to explore them through the lens of evolution: at each stage, as you embody a quality or master an activation, you reset the paradigm soul is expressing and you enable it to expand its experience through you or your business.

You reset and start again at a different level of being; a different awareness of self; a different growth phase within your business.

Soul always meets you where you are; the Signatures activate where you are, supporting your expansion and mastery at that stage before shifting gears to the next level.

If you only focus on the qualities and activations within your four key Signatures - which are the *work* - and t*he practical alignment* to soul, you *will* enable a greater understanding, confidence and reassurance of your path. You will know that you and your business are absolutely supported and guided by soul.

You will start being soul confident. In every single way.

7

UNDERSTANDING THE SIGNATURE ASPECTS

DURING THE NEXT part of this book, you'll be working directly with the Soul Signatures, identifying those relevant to your Soul Signatures Profile and generating an understanding of what that actually means for your life and business. Before we do that, I'd like to walk you through the subheadings within each Signature chapter, so that you are able to make the most of the information shared and differentiate between what the Signatures bring from a personal and business perspective.

In each of their chapters, you'll see the following subheadings:

Archetypal Persona: The 'simple' personality overview linked with that Soul Signatures' energy, highlighting some key characteristics.

Qualities: These are the attributes that soul, through your Signatures, is asking you to be aware of, align with and ultimately embody. These are natural qualities which are present, or available, in your life or business and they form key building blocks which are significant to growth, next-level development or self-awareness. It is just as important to be aware of why and where you are *not* leaning into these qualities, as it is to understand where you are.

These also provide a mechanism for activating a particular Signature, enabling it to be a more dominant, expressive energy.

Activations: Activations are the *work* of the Soul Signatures; characteristics they set in motion. These are gifts and traits for you to cultivate because they empower and authorise.

As with the qualities, you can work with a Signature's activations to support that Signature being more influential.

Soul Prompts: These could also be called challenges! They are the *"ask"* which soul desires you (*prompts* you) to face and master. In doing so, you'll be transcending core sabotaging behaviours or patterns of resistance. You'll also find that it is easier to lean more fully into the Signature's qualities and activations.

Personal: An overview of how the Signature might show up in life, the different ways it could present its energy and suggestions to augur greater harmony.

Business: An overview of how the Signature might demonstrate its energy from a business perspective, ways to work with its guidance and how to support the challenge or growth it offers.

Annual: This section describes the considerations of each Signature from an annual perspective, highlighting direction, opportunities and possible obstacles so that you can navigate your year with greater confidence and ease. From a business perspective, I have just detailed an overarching sentence about what it might be useful for your business to aim for. You can take this deeper as you become more familiar with the Signatures.

You will find that there are some cross-overs between the individual Signatures because they are all part of that energetic dynamic of soul. You are an individual, as is your business and so there will be certain elements of a Signature's overview which *speak* to you more. Trust your intuition first and foremost because this is the voice of soul moving through your energetic structure and enabling its message to be known by you.

Things you might like to consider which will support confidence in the expression of soul with you and through you:

- What common themes arise within your Soul Signatures? Where can you place them within life, challenges and growth?

- Is there an overall energy, intention, or pattern? Can you see the flow, the road that you have walked and why?
- Is there something which is missing? Is this something present that you have shied away from?
- Which feels most true for you and your business right now? (These tend to be Signatures which are particularly active at the present time)
- Which Signatures or Signature qualities feel aspirational?
- Which Signature energy do you hold with ease and which do you need to learn to master?
- Where is the challenge felt more deeply, or more regularly, and does understanding the Signature help you to realise what you are being asked to lean into and how that will serve you?

Finally, you'll see each of the Signature chapters has a brief *italicised* paragraph near the beginning. These are the channelled, energetic vibrational words of the Soul Signatures themselves - they resonate directly with both soul and your energy on a vibrational frequency. These may resonate with you as you read them, or they may make no sense at all - please don't worry if the latter is the case as it is the dynamic of energy which is enabled by these words.

Note: a little word on language. I deliberately use the phrases *within you, with you, for you* and *through you,* which you will see as you move through Being Soul Confident. Soul is not a separate entity from you; it is *part of you* and it desires to *work in partnership with you*. Only by doing so, can it fully enable its expression and energy and support you to its fullest capability.

It works for you because it wants to enable and authorise you, it seeks to work through you (for its own learning and expression). It works within you (to encourage your awareness, intuition and trust for you personally) and it works with you. This partnership enables both its and your fuller potential.

8

IDENTIFYING YOUR SOUL SIGNATURES

BEFORE WE START LOOKING at the actual Soul Signatures and what they mean for your life and business, we need to work them out so you know what they are!

In order, the Soul Signatures are:

1. Initiation
2. Resonance
3. Commitment
4. Anchor
5. Feminine
6. Masculine
7. Emergence
8. Surrender
9. Transformation
10. Integration
11. Devotion

Your Soul Signatures are identified through a numerical process, reducing to a single figure, with the exception of a ten or eleven, to correspond to the specific Signature.

Within Soul Signatures, we don't reduce 10 or 11 as they relate to Signatures themselves. However, I would always recommend incorporating an awareness of Initiation if your Signature is Integration and being aware of the qualities of Resonance if you have a Devotion Signature, as they will be underlying energies which can support you to embody Integration or Devotion more fully.

Let's get started and identify your Soul Signatures - we'll look at your personal Signatures first, before moving on to identifying your business Soul Signatures.

9

YOUR PERSONAL SOUL SIGNATURES

YOUR PERSONAL SIGNATURES are identified as follows:

Foundation Signature Activation This relates to your date of birth - full numbers such as 21/6/1990.

Leading Signature Activation This relates to your <u>full name</u> at birth (include any middle names).

Inner Influence This is identified through your most commonly used name, for instance, your first name or a nickname/ shortened first name. Your inner influence is a *personal* influence.

Please don't use mother or father (or any of their derivatives) as your inner influence - whilst you may be called these most commonly, they are collective rather than personal energies.

Often, we can have a few names that we use and are called by, yet to have, for example, four inner influences defeats the purpose of having an impactful and meaningful Soul Signature influence! The inner influence, as a *personal* influence, is something that you *choose* to align with. My name is Nicola and I use it a lot. I'm also called Nic. I'm happy with that and I do use it, so how do I determine my true inner influence Signature? It is the name that I *choose to use when I am speaking to myself* - "Nic, get a grip", "Nic, that is blooming amazing!" - because that is my most personal connection with my name.

Therefore, Nic is my inner influence; the 'Nicola' Signature will also have aspects that I recognise as influential because it's used regularly. Interestingly Nic has only come into being in the last four or five years. I use Nicola to introduce myself most of the time and I am really comfortable with that as my name. (I did a huge amount of work to own that, which I'll talk about in Part Four because owning your name matters).

Because your inner influence is *a personal choice*, it can also change and evolve as you do: I refused to answer to anything except Niki all through my teenage years and early twenties and I can absolutely see the energy and learning of its Emergence Signature through that period!

External Influence This is identified through a change in name from your leading activation. For example, the introduction of a married name or your full name without the middle name if you have a middle name that you do not use consistently.

If there has been no name change; if your current used full name is the same as your birth name then there is no additional external influence. In this case, your leading activation would be more impactful because the external influence aspect of your profile strengthens your leading activation.

As an added lens, however, you can gently review your surname on its own as an underlying influence. Double-barrelled names, from a Soul Signatures perspective, are always viewed as *one Signature*; the hyphen links them together as a singular aspect, negating individual influences.

10

WORKING OUT YOUR PERSONAL SIGNATURE ACTIVATIONS

ALWAYS USE full numbers and *then* reduce rather than reducing numeric values first and then adding the reductions together. This is the difference between receiving a Devotion Signature or a naturally occurring Resonance Signature and receiving an Integration Signature or a naturally occurring Initiation Signature.

Example - Date of Birth:

2 September 1971

Add whole numbers and *then* reduce: 2 + 9 + 1971 = 1982

which reduces to 20 (1+9+8+2), which reduces to 2 corresponding to a *natural Resonance Signature*

Reducing numbers and then adding: 2 + 9 + 18 (which is the sum of 1+9+7+1) = 29 which reduces to 11, a Devotion Signature.

The accurate Signature activation here is the naturally occurring Resonance Signature, rather than the Devotion Signature.

Working out the Numeric Value of Names

Names are worked out by aligning letters to numbers ranging from 1 to 9, as per the table below:

Numerology Alphabet

1	2	3	4	5	6	7	8	9
A	B	C	D	E	F	G	H	I
J	K	L	M	N	O	P	Q	R
S	T	U	V	W	X	Y	Z	

The numbers corresponding to the name are then added to form the numeric value for that name, which is then reduced to a single digit unless a 10 or 11 is received as these relate to specific Signatures themselves.

Example - Name

G E O R G E   J O H N   S M I T H

7+5+6+9+7+5   1+6+8+5   1+4+9+2+8

= 39   = 20   = 24

For the Leading Signature Activation (which is the FULL name) you would add the numbers as they are and then reduce rather than reducing further and then adding (again this is to ensure that where there is a naturally occurring Initiation or Resonance Signature they are able to be identified)

Therefore: George John Smith would be: 39 + 20 + 24 = 83 which reduces to 11 so George's **leading activation** is Devotion.

His **inner influence** which is his first (or most used name) of George is 39 which reduces to 12, which reduces to 3 = Commitment Signature.

If George's most used name was, for example, Georgie then that would be his inner influence, which would also be a Commitment Signature:

G E O R G I E

7+5+6+9+7+9+5 = 48 which reduces to 12, which reduces to 3, identifying the Commitment Signature.

If he was most commonly called, based on the initials of his first and middle name, GJ then his inner influence would be a Surrender Signature (7 + 1 = 8).

George's **external influence** would be his usual full name: George Smith (let's say he doesn't generally call himself George John Smith except on legal documents).

George Smith (39 + 24 = 63 which reduces to 9) equates to a Transformation Signature so this is his main external influence (as a secondary, subconscious influence, you could reflect on the individual Signature of his surname, Smith, which is a Masculine Signature).

If he did always call himself George John Smith - then his *external influence would be the SAME as his leading activation* and would strengthen that.

Let's assume George John Smith is generally known by George Smith, that his most used name is George, with a date of birth of 2 September 1971.

George's Soul Signatures Profile would be:

Foundation Activation: Resonance Signature

Leading Activation: Devotion Signature

Inner Influence: Commitment Signature

External Influence: Transformation Signature

One final aspect to consider is his middle name, which isn't used (John). This is a Resonance Signature. Now, as this is already present in his foundation activation we don't need to bring this into the mix any further. However, if it had been a different Signature, one which supported his profile as a whole and lent something to his journey through life, we might want to consider suggesting that he activates that Signature by working with it (and I'll talk more about this in Part Four). As the Signature relates to a middle name which isn't used, it is present but underlying rather than actively influencing.

To conclude, your *Foundation and Leading Activations* and your *Inner and External Influences* are the four Soul Signatures to review and consider. Do review them individually and then review them as a whole (in Part Three, I share some case studies to support you in looking at your profile as a whole) so you can gain the wider picture of how soul is guiding your path, influencing your choices, encouraging your growth and enabling confidence and reassurance in who you are and how you are leading your life.

11

YOUR BUSINESS SOUL SIGNATURES

Your business Signatures are identified as follows:

Foundation Signature Activation This relates to the *month and year* you started your *current* business. This does not have to be the specific date you registered it, as your business often starts before you technically put it down on paper. You have generally started to put things in place, developed your concept etc., before you actually register it.

Your business soul shifts with a significant pivot as the focus of your business shifts. Using the month and year of your current business supports understanding the current foundation activation. If your business has shifted its focus significantly, you may choose to review the original foundation activation as it can help you see the shift in soul energy, supporting how you perceive the alignment of your current business in relation to its previous incarnation.

Leading Signature Activation This relates to the *full name* of your business as it is registered for tax purposes or on legal documentation. Please include Limited, Incorporated, Company etc., as part of your business's full name.

Note: If you have changed your business name and your *focused intention* is on the newer name but it is still registered with the original name, then your leading foundation is moving into the new name. Identify both, and use your new name's Signature but be aware that there will still be an underlying influence from the originating Signature whilst that is still its legal name.

Inner Influence The inner influence for your business is *your personal foundation activation*, which responds to your date of birth. It is the inner influence because it is the unchanging, subconscious Signature energy that you bring to your business.

External Influence/s There's potential for *two* external influences from a business perspective. One is identified through *your personal leading activation* because your leading activation lights your way and how soul is leading you influences how you lead your business.

The second external influence comes into play if your business has any nicknames or abbreviated names that are <u>often used</u> - for instance, the British Broadcasting Corporation is more commonly known as the 'BBC' and so the Signature relating to 'BBC' would be an external influence and it would be a strong external influence as 'BBC' is the most commonly known and used name.

Generally, where there are two external influences, the abbreviated business name exerts a stronger influence than your leading activation as this directly relates to the business itself. Your leading activation becomes a secondary or subconscious influence.

If you have more than one abbreviation for your business then its most widely used abbreviation exerts a stronger external influence.

12

WORKING OUT YOUR BUSINESS
SIGNATURE ACTIVATIONS

ALWAYS USE full numbers and then reduce rather than reducing numeric values first and then adding the reductions together. This is the difference between receiving a Devotion Signature or a naturally occurring Resonance Signature and receiving an Integration Signature or a naturally occurring Initiation Signature.

Example - Start Month and Year:

a) June 1992

Add whole numbers and *then* reduce: $6 + 1992 = 1998 = 27$

which reduces to a 9, responding to a Transformation Signature

b) August 1992

Add whole numbers and *then* reduce: $8 + 1992 = 2000$

which reduces to a 2, corresponding to a *natural Resonance Signature*

Reducing numbers and then adding: 8 + 21 (which is the sum of 1+9+9+2) = 29 which reduces to 11, a Devotion Signature.

The accurate Signature activation in example b) is the naturally occurring Resonance Signature, rather than the Devotion Signature.

Working out the Numeric Value of Names

Names are worked out by aligning letters to numbers ranging from 1 to 9, as per the table below:

Numerology Alphabet

1	2	3	4	5	6	7	8	9
A	B	C	D	E	F	G	H	I
J	K	L	M	N	O	P	Q	R
S	T	U	V	W	X	Y	Z	

The numbers corresponding to the name are then added to form the numeric value for that name, which is then reduced to a single digit, unless a 10 or 11 is received as these relate to specific Signatures themselves.

Example - Name

JANE   SMITH   COACHING

1+1+5+5   1+4+9+2+8   3+6+1+3+8+9+5+7

LIMITED*

3+9+4+9+2+5+4

=12   =24   =42   =36

For the Leading Signature Activation (which is the FULL name) you would add the numbers as they are above and then reduce, rather than reducing further first and then adding (again, this is to ensure that where there is a naturally occurring Initiation or Resonance Signature they are able to be identified).

Therefore: Jane Smith Coaching Limited would be: 12 + 24 + 42 + 36 = 114 which reduces to 6; the **_leading activation_** is Masculine.

As they are reduced further, so Jane to 3 (1+2) and so on and then added, they would still enable a Masculine Signature in this instance. *For information, 'Limited' as a word in itself is a Transformation Signature and LTD, the abbreviation, also corresponds to Transformation but always use the full version for your leading activation if it is specified as that because the 36 rather than the reduced 9 can influence the identity of the Signature. If your business is registered as "Ltd" then use that and its numeric correspondence.

The ***inner influence*** for your business would be your personal foundation activation which corresponds to your date of birth. In the example above, let's say that Jane's birth date is 19 September 1973; this would correspond to a Commitment Signature.

One ***external influence*** for Jane Smith Coaching Limited will be *the personal leading activation* (full name at birth). If Jane was Jane Anne Smith at birth then an external influence would be the Emergence Signature.

However, if the business was also known by an abbreviation, such as JS Coaching, an external influence would be the Surrender Signature:

J S Coaching = 1 + 1 + 42 = 44 which reduces to 8 - Surrender

If the business was often simply called JSC then an external influence would be the Feminine Signature (1 + 1 + 3 = 5)

If we have Jane Anne Smith (born 19/9/1973) running Jane Smith Coaching Limited, which is also known as JS Coaching, and it started in August 1992, its Soul Signatures Profile would be:

Foundation Activation: Resonance Signature

Leading Activation: Masculine Signature

Inner Influence: Commitment Signature

External Influences: Surrender *(this is the dominant external influence as it directly relates to the business name)* with a subconscious energy of the Emergence Signature as Jane's own leading activation.

13

ANNUAL SOUL SIGNATURES

ANNUAL SIGNATURES ARE fluid as they change year on year, so they are not included as part of the Soul Signatures profile but they are *very interesting* to review.

Life is guided by external factors which influence us - moon cycles, planetary positions and numerology, for instance, all play their part in influencing our life on a cyclical basis. We feel these influences to a greater or lesser degree depending on our awareness and where things are activated or 'triggered' within life.

Soul, as well as being a personal energy working specifically with us, forms part of a divine whole. That whole influences the universal energy and everything which is part of it.

Understanding its influence and cycles through an annual perspective can help us to meet the universal soul energies impacting life and work with them for our benefit. And when you identify your personal or business annual Signatures as well, you can really harness the natural energy flow each year brings by directly leaning into the specific growth, development, healing or expansion soul is gifting through that annual Signature cycle.

Universal Annual Signatures

Each year has a universal annual Signature and it is very simply the year itself reduced to a single digit (unless a 10 or 11) and related to the corresponding Signature.

2023 is an Emergence Year - $2 + 0 + 2 + 3 = 7$

2024 is a Surrender Year - $2 + 0 + 2 + 4 = 8$

Universal annual Signatures are the overarching energy for everyone, so even with a different personal annual Signature, look at that, if you can, through the lens of it also being influenced by the universal Signature because you are part of, and impacted by, the universal energies and this will support you in understanding the subtler nuances of your personal annual Signature. (If it is a bit too much to integrate initially, focus on your personal Signature because that *is* personal to you.)

In identifying how influenced you are by an annual Signature, it can be useful to look back at the previous year; we often see the lessons and learning more clearly with hindsight.

2022 was a Masculine year. It brought the awareness that structure, strategy, process and discipline support you and support growth. In very simplistic terms, you will have found that where structure and discipline were in place, you achieved and where they weren't, focus and progress were more difficult.

Reviewing the last annual Signature and recognising its energy can help you to commit to the current year's Signature because it builds faith and confidence.

Your Personal Annual Signature

Your personal annual Signature runs from your birthday to your next birthday. It doesn't follow the pattern of January to December because that is not your annual cycle.

Your personal annual Signature is worked out using your day and month of birth in line with the current year and then linking that with your birth date (your foundation activation).

Let's use our fictitious Jane Smith as our example:

Jane's date of birth is 19 September 1973 which equates to 2001 (with everything Signature-based, remember to *keep whole numbers and then reduce*)

If we want to know the Signature for 2023 we use Jane's day and month of birth with the year we are identifying the Signature for, so:

19 September 2023, which gives us 2051

<u>We then ADD this to the whole DOB number of 2001</u>:

2051 + 2001 = 4052 which reduces to 11.

Therefore from Jane's birthday in September 2023 to her birthday in 2024, she will be influenced by a personal annual Signature of Devotion.

Let's have a look at how we can view Devotion through the lens of the universal annual Signatures:

During 2023 she will be influenced universally by Emergence which, as you will see in Part Two, is about vision and growth. And in 2024 she'll be influenced by Surrender which is about purpose and service, as well as collaboration.

Devotion is about mastery and leadership so, on a personal level, Jane will be challenged to step into leading her life, gaining mastery over certain elements of it and herself. Universally, she is being asked to step into a bigger vision as she moves through 2023 because in 2024 there is an energy which asks about purpose and service - making life and what you do within it matter.

To meet those universal elements, the Devotion Signature is asking Jane to master those parts of life and within herself (e.g. mindset, discipline, emotional mastery) that she needs to in order to step into aspects of leadership and move into being a leader; both a bigger vision and a stronger or more focused purpose will require leadership.

Your Business Annual Signature

In the same way that your personal annual Signature runs from birthday to birthday so too does your business's yearly Signature. And it is worked out in exactly the same way, aligning with the foundation activation for your business.

If we use Jane Smith's business foundation activation it is:

August 1992 = 2000 (remember whole numbers and then reduce)

For 2023, we use the month of August and 2023 which equates to: 2031

We then <u>ADD 2031 to the foundation number of 2000</u>, giving us: 4031 which reduces to 8 and is a Surrender Signature.

Therefore, from August 2023 to July 2024, the annual Signature influence for Jane Smith Coaching is Surrender - Purpose, Service and Collaboration.

This indicates that Jane's business will benefit by looking at its purpose and really digging deep into what change it wants to engender within the world and how it can serve in a more meaningful way. It is also a great year for collaborating or partnering with others, as long as the purpose/ vision aligns.

<u>Note:</u> I don't advocate using the universal annual Signature as an overarching influence within businesses as we tend to be more impacted by universal energies on a personal level,

so I would suggest reading your annual business Signature as a stand-alone aspect.

Before we move further and start learning about the Signatures themselves, I'd like to offer some guidance:

- Before reading any information about any Signature, just spend a moment looking at the Signature itself. Be aware of any insights, awareness or feelings which arise.
- There is *a lot* of information contained within these pages. Take your time and initially read the Soul Signatures within your profile as individual Signatures rather than trying to link all four as a whole profile picture - let that come after you have digested the Signatures individually.
- Make notes about those aspects you read which you feel through every fibre of your being - things you simply *know* to be true. These form the **fundamental truths** of those Signatures for you specifically, so they matter. Make notes about anything else which resonates or that you find interesting.
- Look at the qualities and activations. Which do you already lean into, embody and own? Celebrate that. Your work is to develop (or develop further) the other qualities and other activations so they are embodied and can be relied upon.

- Note anything which triggers you as you read it. These are likely to be things that you need to be aware of and bring to healing or neutrality within you.
- If you can, take some time between Signatures to simply create space. Perhaps do some journalling and just allow whatever rises. The Signatures are relatable and practical in their qualities but they are also energetic and energy has its own language which moves through you, so give it the space to do so.

Whilst there are specific qualities and activations within each Signature, some will be more present, notable and noticeable through your life or your business than others. How soul *speaks* to you will be individual and perfect for you and for your receptivity of its energy. I've used the quality of resourcefulness with Integration; you may feel resilience is more apt as a consistent quality for you. Whilst they are different, there are similarities so trust yourself if a slightly different quality or activation, *but with strong similarities*, is more resonant.

PART II

THE SOUL SIGNATURES

14

INITIATION

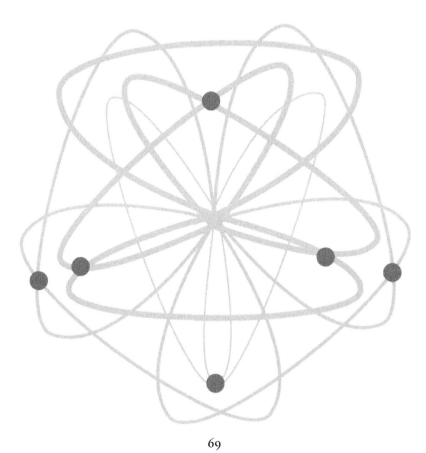

INITIATION IS the beginning and all of its renewals. Every journey and each moment offer initiations into new opportunities and potential as yet unknown.

Within every aspect of soul comes myriad moments of initiation into new, bolder and truer aspects of being.

The activation of the Initiation Signature is an acknowledgement of a new path or potential opening, aligned with and supported by soul.

Archetypal Persona The Innovator

The Innovator desires to be different and to do things differently. A refusal to conform, a deep desire to push boundaries, to challenge generalised thinking or recognised ways of living and being within life, all speak to the Innovator.

Initiation supports the ability to naturally start over with optimism and idealism. Fear of failure does not worry the Innovator as much as being trapped in routine or a regularity which stifles curiosity, independence and a yearning to explore life fully.

Qualities Innovation, Direction, Curiosity

Innovation leads, lending the opportunity to innovate, to think on one's feet and snatch triumph, or at least possibility, out of challenge or failure.

Direction is important, as are changes of direction. Whilst there is a clear desire to do things your way, you achieve more when that is directed with a purpose or destination in mind, as long as there is a level of fluidity.

Curiosity brings the desire to explore beyond boundaries, an impulse to try new things, an openness to new ideas and cultures and the courage to say "what if...". Curiosity can feel limited by the need to have a direction of travel and yet it creates the vehicle for innovation to find its form.

Blending innovation with curiosity can shape a natural and purposeful direction, enabling you to harness opportunity which continually evolves.

Activations Adaptability, Resourcefulness, Trust

Moving away from certainty inspires innovation; the ability to think and act swiftly develops adaptability in changing situations and circumstances - a skill you can develop and learn to trust.

Innovation takes you out of your comfort zone - treading new ground and being willing to create a new path requires a deep level of trust and the ability to cultivate levels of resourcefulness that you had not realised nor anticipated, and can prevent remaining within the compelling lure of familiarity.

Trust in yourself and the ability to navigate a changeable and evolving path develops with a greater sense of resource-fulness and the knowledge that you can adapt to changing situations - situations which directly facilitate these skills' development and situations which test the trust you hold in yourself by asking you to put all of your eggs in one basket - your basket.

Soul Prompts Surrender Expectations and Allow

Initiation's soul prompt asks you to surrender how you think life is going to be or should be so that you can meet the moment *in* the moment, with everything you need at your disposal at that moment in time.

Stepping upon any new path requires a sense of direction, resolve and trust and yet, it is only as you step upon the path that what is awaiting you makes itself known. Initiation asks you to be open to what you may find as you walk along a different avenue, to allow what you may not have considered, secure in the knowledge that you can meet any circumstance with the necessary adaptability and innovation to succeed and flourish.

Personal

Foundation Activation: Initiation permeates life with a desire to be innovative. Change and challenges arise which stretch you to think outside of the box and to try different ideas, concepts or approaches to directly build the muscle of innovation, strengthen your resourcefulness and the ability you have to trust yourself to adapt to life and whatever it may deliver your way.

Stagnation and routine stifle you; curiosity lends itself to exploration and so, Initiation not only encourages innovation through life but also for you to reach outside of societal boundaries and push beyond the limits of what might be probable to discover what is possible.

It is important to remember that a direction of travel supports you; it can be used as a tool to begin a journey however, rather than as a definitive destination to aim for.

Innovation will always bring you back to being curious about how you can do things, or do you, differently. If you can view a challenge with a curiosity and perspective which explores it as a gift, you will directly inspire innovation.

Leading Activation: You are being asked to *learn* the skills that enable you to innovate with ease and move into being more curious about engaging with life. You're encouraged to step into being comfortable with adaptability, empowering a greater sense of resourcefulness so that you are able to step into the unknown with trust in your ability to meet the needs of the moment with curiosity.

As you master the ability to shift and adapt with more ease as life asks you to embrace growth, opportunity presents itself - often in a way you had not anticipated and it is the quiet confidence of trust within yourself, and your ability to draw on resourcefulness, which turns the key, allowing you to walk into new adventures and more expansive potential.

Be curious and willing to move your awareness away from what you know and expect, and life will open directions of travel which offer a different, but more fulfilling and exciting potential.

As both Foundation and Leading Activations: The ability and need to innovate are essential. Pushing boundaries is an intrinsic desire that, if met with trust and belief in your ability to meet any situation with curiosity and adaptability, can create and lead to living life fully on your terms.

Generally, challenges arise when you hold yourself back or are unable to follow through, leading to a lack of trust in yourself and your ability to meet life's ask. Stagnation and routine are the total antithesis of innovation and can lead to you feeling constrained and restricted.

It is vital that you learn to trust yourself, your decision-making and your ability to be resourceful. As opportunities and potential call, you need to meet those and lead with curiosity to explore both life and yourself, reassured that you can always adapt and innovate to attain fulfilment and success on your terms.

Business

Foundation Activation: This lends your business the ability to innovate and adapt, to meet the needs of the moment and of change in climate or culture more easily and, as such, assists its longevity.

Navigating with Initiation encourages your business to explore how it can remain current, meaningful and relevant by doing things differently.

Resourcefulness and adaptability support your business's strength and resilience; it can mean that there are opportunities for growth and risk-taking which would otherwise not be considered.

Remember that the soul of your business is seeking to innovate, and whilst change meets all businesses at some stage, Initiation indicates a need to actively seek opportunities to do things differently, suggesting that challenges which arise will do so to encourage your business to consider how it *can* innovate - a perspective worth noting in times of challenge.

Leading Activation: Initiation suggests actively looking for ways to innovate in your business's industry, and to break new ground in what it does and how it does it. Your business has the potential to incorporate different concepts, expand into different territories and encourage curiosity and variety.

Resourcefulness and an aptitude for adaptability are required. Innovation requires courage, and that courage must originate from the skills at the heart of your business.

Identifying what does, or could, make your business (more) resourceful, and understanding how adaptable it is can support its ability to innovate in times of change.

Generally, whilst trust is an activation of Initiation, within a business, it relates to trust in your systems and key players. Without trust in the foundational processes which enable efficiency and ease, it becomes difficult to gain the freedom of thought, and time, to truly allow creativity and innovation.

Annual

Initiation asks you to do things differently and be curious about what comes next. New potential or opportunity presents itself, encouraging one to explore a different path or perspective.

New beginnings are a definitive energy with Initiation, so where things are stagnant, unchanging or stuck, expect there to be challenges or changes which leave no room for staying the same. Actively cutting the deadwood can help you to step in and make the most of this Signature's potential and activation.

Whatever begins or is initiated this year has momentum; it asks you to act and flow with the tide, trusting in your ability to adapt, be resourceful and innovate to meet life.

Business Perspective: Where can you innovate and do things differently to support either expansion or sustainability? If different opportunities call or are offered, Initiation suggests curiosity and a desire to explore their potential.

An annual Initiation Signature can also see the start of a business or the start of a new business alongside a current one. There is momentum to this energy, suggesting a good opportunity as long as adaptability and the ability to be resourceful can be met in the early stages.

15

RESONANCE

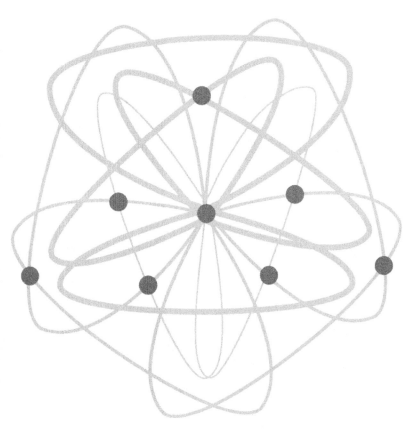

RESONANCE IS the dynamic energy which cultivates a greater belief, deeper self-trust and the realisation of being part of a greater whole.

Within every aspect of soul we evolve as it expands through us, its frequency reaching a greater resonance and influencing beyond our boundaries.

The activation of the Resonance Signature is confirmation of the opening of the portals of time and an understanding of your soul's eternal nature.

Archetypal Persona The Believer

The Believer inhabits the sure and certain knowledge that they are part of a greater whole and that the energy brought into life on a daily basis is reflected back to them. There is an innate belief that anything is possible, lending conviction to an aligned path; yet it must be underpinned by doing the work of self - of mindset, of growth and courageous action to really manifest.

Resonance ingrains a deep sense of the connectedness of all life; the need to feel in flow and aligned is paramount. This can bring a challenge when life doesn't appear to flow easily because it can start to unravel the belief one has in a pathway or self.

Qualities Belief, Flow, Aligned Energy

Belief is a fundamental that must be mastered with this Signature; finding the seed of belief in yourself, and in life, which is true, real and unshakeable no matter the situation or circumstance. If you can believe it (and believe in yourself to achieve it), it is possible.

Flow matters. Flow enables productivity and a sense of progress. It supports belief in yourself and belief in what you are aiming for; motivation can be difficult to maintain without a sense of flow. Being in flow supports aligned energy and aligned energy supports flow.

Being aligned energetically, feeling that harmony of energy within yourself, your values and beliefs and how you are living that within life, creates momentum, opportunity and zeal which makes everything possible, probable and achievable and every challenge surmountable.

Resonance impresses you to recognise the difference between what you think you believe and what you do believe so that you can move past the mind, into the sensitivity of energy and know yourself *beyond your thoughts about yourself*.

Activations Universal Awareness, New Possibilities

The specific energetic frequency of Resonance means that it activates awareness beyond you as an individual. A sensitivity to yourself as part of the universal picture influences what you do in life, how you do it and the impact or influence you wish to bring to the world, or your world.

As Resonance is activated within your soul presence, you recognise yourself as a cog in the larger wheel of life.

As this understanding of universal awareness grows, different possibilities arise that were not possible before and horizons which were not even in view, suddenly become visible.

Soul Prompts Release Limiting Mindscts

The limitation within any aspect of energy is what you believe to be true or possible. Resonance is a direct request to do the work to release the limitations which you place on yourself through the mindset and behaviours you hold.

Every time you gain awareness from an energetic perspective; every time your energy vibration shifts or expands, you meet resistance (at a different level) which you will need to overcome. As you do, you gain a greater level of energetic acuity with the flow state being more present, more fully enabling deeper alignment within yourself and life.

As you expand energetically, you eventually reach the next set point from a limitation perspective where further mindset work is required.

Personal

Foundation Activation: Resonance will always bring you back to feeling aligned - within yourself, with where you are in life, with what you are doing and how you are doing it. The more aligned you feel, the more congruence between all aspects of your being and life, and the more you meet life with vigour and undiminished belief in what is possible.

If you can master your energetic awareness, you will be able to build upon unshakeable foundations. Life can feel as if it is against you when you are not aligned, creating a sense of constraint and impacting through lowering your mental and emotional resilience.

Belief in yourself and what is possible can be a natural given to a certain extent. Manifesting it requires you to address limiting mindsets; belief is a knowing which meets its energetic resistance and requires you to align the whole. There will be a dance between energy and mindset, between mindset and energy; sustaining your flow state is what takes the work.

Leading Activation: Resonance suggests that bringing a greater level of energetic awareness to your life will support a sense of flow and enable you to feel as though life, and yourself, are in an aligned space. A greater sense of purpose and fulfilment can be found and there is an ease which creates opportunity, opening potential and new possibilities for you.

Recognise that when life 'opens', you are in flow. The more you can start to tap into this, the more impact you will be able to make in your own life and within life.

When you feel aligned, belief is empowered because it is able to cut through the 'noise' of life - belief which is felt through all of your awareness, supporting trust in yourself and your possibilities, and the ability to take aligned action.

Resonance asks you to look at where limiting beliefs are holding you back from achievement, success or fulfilment and do the work to release these, cultivating beliefs, mindset and emotional states which support you to stand in authority within yourself and life.

As both Foundation and Leading Activation: Energy really is everything and it is essential that you both understand and master the ability to refine your own energy in all areas, and move into the state which serves you at any given moment in time.

Your ability to be in an aligned state can literally manifest opportunities or change of all sorts. In the same way, the lack of ability to master your own energy can keep you stuck in patterns of behaviour or situations within life that drain and disempower you, making change difficult and the belief which is required to enable change hard to sustain.

Generally, Resonance guides you to the understanding that your world is a reflection of your inner self and that you can change your world by changing your inner landscape. Because energy always expands, you will always meet your own resistance and this is where you need to commit to looking at that resistance and working through and beyond it.

It is much easier to maintain a consistent energetic hygiene routine than it is to keep having to build one back up when things fall down. If you can support your energy awareness and energy state through disciplined practices, then you will reap their benefit time and again, being able to easily shift back into a better state when life throws curve balls or challenges to test you or to engender growth.

Business

Foundation Activation: Resonance indicates that your business needs to feel aligned as a whole. There needs to be a congruence between different elements, different arms or different offers or services within the business. Whilst many businesses do well diversifying, any diversification needs to align with the core promise or values of the business.

There can often be an unshakeable belief that your business will work, thrive and succeed and this lends a drive and a vision which subconsciously supports its success. Don't let this belief allow you to negate the need to do the work which supports business in general.

Your business is built on the foundations of releasing its limitations in terms of growth. As its energy as a whole is aligned, so it has the potential and foundational support to move through perceived limitations within its industry or area of expertise and create new benchmarks.

Leading Activation: You are asked to ensure your business, its offers, message and purpose are aligned and congruent. Enabling your business to be aligned encourages cohesiveness and coherence within all its aspects, engenders a sense of flow and enables a clearer sense of direction, purpose and vision.

Trying to do too many different things, with different objectives, varying visions or aims lends a sense of a business which doesn't know what it is or what it is here to do. Without a sense of purpose, it can become difficult for belief to hold it steady in challenge or change.

As a business owner, Resonance asks you to look at the limitations within your business or team - for instance, what skills need to be developed or what work could be outsourced? Whilst releasing limited mindsets is a personal ask of the Resonance Signature (and it absolutely does relate to you or team members as individuals) from a business perspective it asks you to be mindful of its limitations so that you can find a way to mitigate them.

Whether Resonance is a foundation or leading activation, it specifically empowers aligned energy and a flow within, and of, the business. The more you can enable this, the greater ability you lend your business to expand and express itself as an authority within its field, as a business people can rely on and believe in.

Annual

Resonance asks you to focus on where things are aligned, where they aren't and to enable a better sense of alignment to permit more flow and so that belief (or self-belief) has the opportunity and space to step forward and be realised.

A Resonance year is one to do all of the work around subconscious beliefs and mindset so that energy is able to flow unrestricted. Understanding energy differently, being more sensitive to it and owning your belief about what might be possible if energy was aligned are key areas where Resonance makes its influence felt.

It asks you to look outside of yourself to see more than yourself, and in doing so, you are more able to recognise the bigger picture - thereby diminishing insignificant issues or a narrow viewpoint and creating a different conversation.

Personal energy practices are also highlighted.

Business Perspective: Resonance directs you to bring different elements of your business together as a whole, so the business feels aligned and so that you feel aligned and reconnected to it in a deeper, more centred way. Where your business doesn't have different aspects to align, this year challenges how aligned you feel to it and its purpose; it asks you to ensure you are aligned as you move forward and your business grows.

16

COMMITMENT

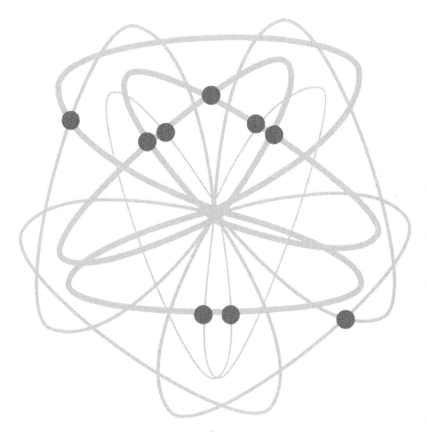

COMMITMENT IS the moment where truth can no longer be denied. As it is understood more fully, it expresses through word, act and deed.

Within every aspect of soul arrives the specific moment that we are asked to commit to its creative, courageous and determined vitality and to ourselves.

The activation of the Commitment Signature is a calling for a commitment to nothing less than your total truth.

Archetypal Persona The Communicator

The Communicator wants to share who they are. Through understanding themselves, their truth and their deepest essence, the Communicator gains the confidence to express that with courage and clarity, moving past the fear of judgement in that expression.

Commitment supports the ability to progress through standing in the power of truth because everything aligns - what is said, what is done and what is lived.

As well as learning to know and allow their own truth, other people standing in truth also matter. Dishonesty is a very hard thing for the Communicator to accept in others and overcoming its subtleties within themselves is essential.

Qualities Truth, Discernment, Progress

Truth is Commitment's leading quality. Truth changes and the ability to move deeper, enabling truth at that level, whilst also seeking to express it opens the way for greater freedom. The ability to witness oneself is inherent within this.

Understanding your truth and discerning between that and *the* truth is also something Commitment seeks to distinguish and give confidence in.

Discernment lends the ability to recognise what matters and supports the right choice from the opportunities and paths available; choices that sit within what you feel as truth and contribute to its and your greater understanding and freer expression. Be discerning in where you place your focus and growth, remembering that focus narrows the opportunities but enables mastery within those, sustaining the potential of liberation into your fullest self.

Life expands when truth is owned, acknowledged and becomes the foundation one builds upon. It creates freedom and enables a more expansive potential to be met. Progress is attained through honest reflection and a willingness to lead from that, no matter what the area of self or life.

Activations Courageous Expression, Truth of Self, Clear Sight

Courageous expression is activated because your truth requires it. The ability to be courageous in your expression, speak your truth, stand within it and allow it to guide your voice, energy and actions are the work of Commitment.

Accepting both light and shadow through honest reflection activates truth of self. In knowing yourself, you allow the essential attribute of your light; you cannot live in truth if the truth of your own light is not accepted, allowed and emanates. The quality of your light is defined by the depths to which you are willing to embrace examining your recesses and shadows.

When you know who you are, what is for you and what is not becomes clear. Clear sight activates with Commitment and its power is within recognising the wrong path, the wrong choice and being able to redirect, course correct and transform. Clarity replaces indecision, overwhelm and procrastination.

Soul Prompt Detach from Judgement, Illusion and Fear

Commitment's soul prompt recognises that for truth to surface and lead, you need to be able to know it and voice it freely, compassionately and confidently; in order to do so, you need to be free from the fear or judgement which constrains what you are willing to say and how you say it.

Knowing your truth, and letting that be the certainty which rises and guides your way, disables the illusion of life or yourself and allows you to see things as they are; the perspective which enables progress.

Commitment asks that you detach from judgement, illusion and fear by trusting in who you are, refraining from people pleasing and identifying through others' expectations; courage in the expression of your truth lights the path.

Personal

Foundation Activation: Commitment insists you stand in your personal truth at all times, verifying that your ability to do this can define you positively or negatively. By enabling honest awareness within yourself and exhibiting that through expression and deed, you stand in freedom, for truth is always what sets you free and gifts the conviction of your path. Mastering the nuances of expression is required.

An unshakeable certainty in what is right (and right for you) supports confident assertion as you develop through life and a desire to not just stand in your own truth, but to understand the truth within life.

Exploration of the mind, the longing to understand life and its meaning, which can also assist you to understand yourself more fully, can dictate how you employ your skills, but in all things, if you can be discerning with your choices rather than follow every idea, inspiration and possibility, you will enable the focus required to achieve more and to attain that which fulfils you.

Progress is achieved through living a life which matters to you and which is truthful. In fostering a culture of personal honesty, self-reflection and a willingness to look at all of yourself in the mirror, a natural personal leadership arises.

In consistently aligning to truth, you bring all of yourself to the table, unfolding all of your layers and identifying the core essence which makes you who you are. A fundamental ability to engage with who you are through committed personal development will always reward you.

Leading Activation: Commitment calls you to know yourself so fully that you can never un-know who you are again. Standing in your truth and allowing yourself fully is no longer optional. As you evolve through life, success and achievement mean less if you do not feel fulfilled and are not being true to yourself and your values.

What doesn't serve a purpose aligned with truth becomes a burden which grows heavy to carry. You will be asked to stand up for your beliefs, to move against the crowd and there will be times when you find you are walking life's path alone. The courage of your convictions calls you to stand in impressive integrity and light the way forward.

Discernment within partnerships and friendships is important as the people around you will either support or hinder, celebrate or discourage, and you will always be immeasurably more liberated by the former.

Learning to express who you are, fully and vulnerably, is the growth path. Stepping outside of your comfort zone and detaching from what is expected so that you can enable what is needed are the learnings you need to meet so that you can find freedom within simply being who you are.

As both Foundation and Leading Activation: Truth is both the foundation and the leading light, but it is essential to maintain the realisation that truth changes. Your truth will change as you know yourself more fully and as life offers its experiences to you.

Detaching from judgment and judging can be harder with both activations because your own expectations are high. You stand in the authority of your truth but different people meet challenges where they are rather than where you would meet them yourself.

Generally, progress will always happen when you let go of expectations and simply meet yourself where you are at any given moment. The more you can surrender to who you are and allow everyone else to be as they are, the more you will find freedom. For you, remember it is your truth that matters for in the moment, it is the only truth.

Business

Foundation Activation: Your business has to stand in sovereign truth and lead from that so it must know what it is, what it does and why. Once those fundamentals are solid, commitment to them becomes the root which grounds your business, enabling its trunk to be solid and its branches to reach high.

Business is bold; it is not afraid to speak with directness and honesty and it is not afraid to say no. In different areas of the business or partnerships, there must be a familial ground which aligns with its central truth - its reason for being, and its existential reason for being has to serve a purpose which supports truth within its industry; there has to be more to your business's 'why'.

As your business grows, as it expands or as its reach and opportunities widen, be discerning and ensure it remains rooted in its mission. Fulfilling that or widening that aim, whilst remaining true to the essence, brings a sense of centred progress; progress otherwise may seem scattered or disparate, without providing the stability which is needed.

Leading Activation: As your business develops, it will seek to find its greater meaning which can bring changes of direction or a refocussing or repurposing. As it develops, it knows itself more and it seeks to stand in that truth. Change should not be feared; when it is right, you will feel the truth of it through every fibre of your being.

Once a clear, or different, sense of purpose is established, progress is swift and with courageous expression as an activation, your business seeks to be known rather than stand shyly in the shadows. It wants to express its value and bring meaning to its marketplace.

Detaching from any sense of fear of being judged by peers can be a challenge to overcome and there has to be an unwavering commitment to truth in everything it does.

Be discerning in growth choices, with directions or opportunities. The more you stay within the narrower lens of the core 'why' of your business, the more expansive its opportunities are. Don't be afraid to say "no", for a "no" will always contribute to a better "yes" at a later stage.

Whether a foundation or leading activation, with Commitment, truth always seeks to express itself, so know that your business has a purpose that it wishes to be known for, a purpose which will bring it into the lens of the media or into the gaze of its peers because it believes in what it offers and it wants to enable a wider voice.

Annual

Commitment requires you to look at what aligns with your truth within life, what doesn't, and to transform as required so that you are living, breathing and being in truth.

There is the opportunity for a deeper connection with purpose and greater fulfilment in how you meet life. Knowing who you are now is an essential component. You are asked to meet yourself with truth, and honour and with a commitment to seeing and allowing all of yourself. How you speak to yourself and how you receive yourself can change how you connect with yourself.

If something doesn't serve or support the truth of your nature, this is the year to change it as progress can be made in every area that you meet with openness and courage.

As the Communicator, you can find a deeper expression, a way to understand yourself more deeply and to communi-

cate that to your world, or to the world with greater influence, impact and relevance.

Business Perspective: Commitment asks your business to stand
fully in its truth, own its vision and commit to it with everything it says and does. It may need to speak up or speak out.
It may need to challenge culture, limitations or stigma within
itself or its industry but this will set its foundations firmly and
fully in its purpose and offer greater freedom and
opportunity.

17

ANCHOR

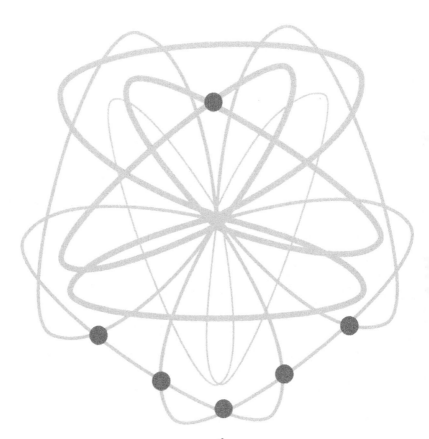

ANCHOR IS the stability that is known and created from within through reinvention, detachment from identity and the awareness of divinity.

Within every aspect of soul we reach a moment of choice, for we can no longer unknow what is now known within.

The activation of the Anchor Signature is a requirement to embed vibrational shifts through identifying with your divinity rather than your individuality.

Archetypal Persona The Change-Maker

The Change-Maker reinvents the self as deeper levels of awareness, truth and being are discovered, meeting change head-on, secure in the knowledge that ending always initiates birth and the permeable essence of life will always win through.

Anchor empowers growth through deep inner change; the ability to take risks and release who one was to permit who one is and wants to be.

Consistency and commitment can feel restraining, even when desired, with wider stability often found through divine connection and a recognition of their place in the greater world. The Change-Maker would rather disrupt than allow a status quo which limits.

Qualities Reinvention, Growth, Creativity

Anchor's ability to engineer reinvention brings reassurance and resilience, a certain knowledge of the opportunity to thrive. Mastering the courage to allow reinvention is a quality that one either grows into or has to learn to hold with trust. It is worth remembering that reinvention is not normally small changes but rather seismic shifts which simply do not allow the present state of affairs to remain.

Growth is enabled through letting go of that which no longer works or supports, no matter how reassuring it may be, and creating change even if the outcome of that change is not known or certain at initiatory stages; creating change because there is an instinctive understanding that stagnation arises from remaining the same and stagnation is the death of creativity and curiosity.

There is fulfilment through creative pursuits or avenues and finding creative solutions to change and growth pathways. Empowering a sense of trust in creative ability, within the circumstances and challenges it brings, leads to meeting reinvention more easily.

Activations Universal Consciousness, Embracing Change, Creativity

Universal consciousness activates an awareness that life is more than is realised; something more than the individuality of self, belonging to a greater whole. As you start to understand this within yourself, the ability to embrace change within yourself and life becomes easier. Indeed, it becomes necessary as there is a desire to meet yourself more fully as you move through life.

Integrating the concept of universal consciousness through life directly supports developing trust within yourself and the process of life as it embeds the ability to embrace change as a constant. Security and stability then start to be realised irrespective of change.

Creativity imbues growth; growth seeks creative solutions. Fitting into the normal solutions and scenarios of life is not for Anchor although creativity will seek a frame in which it can find its form, it is more often than not abstract.

Soul Prompt Shed Who You No Longer Are

Through childhood, adolescence and through societal expectations, an identity is built around whom you believe you 'should' be. Anchor imparts a mission to discover who you truly are, divinely. You do that by being willing to shed aspects of self that you no longer identify with and with which you no longer wish to define yourself.

The more you know yourself, the more of yourself becomes available to be known, therefore, the ability to shed identities no longer relevant, current or desired is a practice you move more deeply into.

The less you can hold onto identity, the more opportunity and space you create to actually know yourself. With Anchor, you are both everything and nothing.

Personal

Foundation Activation: The ability to move through reinvention, enabling liberation into the fullness of self, is inherent within you and situations arise to trigger this. They can feel like dark nights of the soul, each unfoldment into a truer essence requires the death of the previous self and the brutal honesty, and courage, to face yourself fully.

Viewing these as a journey to light rather than a journey through darkness aids each in being simpler to navigate, facilitating the move back into a centred certainty with greater ease.

Identification with the self and a desire to belong create separation; you lose yourself every single time. When you can identify with divine or higher aspects of self, even through immense changes, you retain a sense of belonging to yourself rather than having a need to belong.

Anchor encourages introspection and an exploration of who you are - creativity is a natural tool you can use whether as an art form, through endeavours or through thought processes and the way you understand the world and your-self within it, which are often abstract. Creativity enables you to be in flow; disconnected from self and connected to a more universal consciousness which helps you to witness life from an objective lens; it can also lessen the intensity with which you view yourself and life.

Anchor will always impress a deeper understanding of yourself, which is the catalyst for reinventing how you show up in your life and in the world.

Leading Activation: Anchor instigates a requirement to move into the potential for growth available through personal reinvention and calls you to a path of radical self-awareness and self-reflection; finding a way to sustain that and participate in life fully and confidently is a learning curve.

Whilst reinventing the self might appear to be an act which separates rather than unites the self, energetic and vibrational shifts seek to find their balance through who you actually are rather than who you believe yourself to be.

Anchor always encourages you forward; growth initiates and once it does, it cannot be undone for it cannot be unknown. Cultivating trust within the process of change supports you in finding stability within yourself rather than looking for it externally, and it directly supports being able to embrace change and meet it.

Creativity is your saviour - the more you can lean into creative expression or creative solutions, the more connected you will feel to the sense of self that is sustained through change (the aspect of the divine self) and this facilitates change integrating with more ease.

As both Foundation and Leading Activation: Deep personal change is a given; the more you can appreciate this as serving you and lean into its opportunities for reinvention and growth, the easier you will find navigating life and yourself within it. Stripping back all aspects of identity keeping you separated from a sense of divine connectedness within yourself supports security and stability that expresses from self, rooting you in who you are and giving you the permission and freedom to explore everything you might be.

Generally, an understanding that you are not being less but more of who you are, that a deeper sense of your divinity enables a greater sense of the individuality that you are here to gift to life in all its forms, is part of your soul purpose. Creativity gives you a tool to know yourself outside of the expectations of life's identity.

Anchor also gifts empathy - something you can bring to your life and your work.

Business

Foundation Activation: With the innate ability to reinvent itself, your business directly creates sustainability because of its adaptability and driving change from the ground up. As your business develops it will seek to meet the needs of the moment and market, flexing with the demands of its area of service in order to meet the potential it knows is available.

Creativity is essential because reinvention calls for solutions that are not as obvious or as structured as one might like. The ability to be creative within your business - in design, vision and in the moment - will directly support the potential of your business to be a successful and sustainable enterprise.

Anchor can challenge your belief in what stability within your business actually is and whether it equates to freedom or constraint. Being brave enough to believe in what you are creating and then allowing it to find its ultimate form and service directly authorises the Signature.

Think of Anchor as bringing all aspects to the table so that your business can be seen and known in all its glory. Through its iterations, it will find a sense of purpose and achievement which enables it to be so much more than the vision you originally held and it will take you on that journey with it.

Leading Activation: Anchor asks your business to be willing to lean into change. Whatever its vision in its beginning, it seeks its ultimate identity (purpose) and it will move through change and reinvention until it finds it.

Being balanced with where you place limits, and knowing why they are in place, supports sustainable change. As your business seeks what it knows it is capable of achieving, it will want to let go of what holds it back so you will find that foundational aspects of your business will ask to be released in order to create new ground, new ideas and new energy. This is essential for it to meet and sustain change within its profession and remain current.

The foundation activation will determine what best supports a business with a leading Anchor activation and if you can use its support, you will enable a confident, aligned business which changes to fulfil a wonderful purpose and is able to meet change within its profession with confident ease.

The more that you can allow your business to serve in the moment, the more you will enable it to meet its own potential and fulfil its purpose.

Annual

Anchor is a year of reinvention where you are asked to embrace the opportunity of change. Whether within one's self or in life, it is no longer possible to let things stay as they are. Anchor brings this to the fore and makes it non-negotiable. Embracing change will create greater ease than resisting it and the more creative and open you can be through mindset - seeing change as growth - the greater clarity and confidence you will have in the next steps you need to take.

Knowing that you are moving forward allows you to release what is needed, whether within yourself or in life; it is essential you keep moving forward, for the outcome will not be apparent in the moment.

Trust in a higher purpose can sustain the steps forward, and in part, Anchor will be about cultivating a refined connection to your divine self; if you can remember that it is about bringing more of yourself to your life, you will find it easier to reflect and hold witness to the change which is occurring and allow it.

Business Perspective: Anchor encourages your business to be open to and creative with change. There are possibilities for change, some of which may be radical but which will absolutely support your business's stability and potential for longevity. Trust in you and your business's ability to be resourceful and adapt to the needs of the market or the time.

18

FEMININE

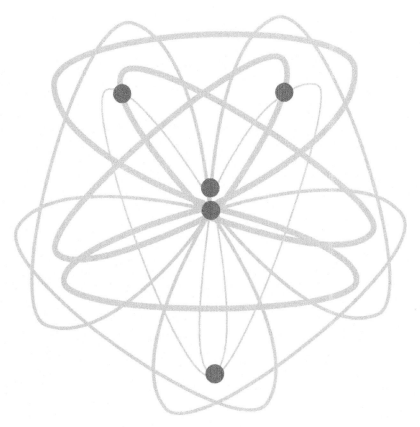

THE **FEMININE** IS the majesty of energetic balance authorising the leadership of empowered intuition through the emergence of a deeper self.

Within every aspect of soul is a perfect and harmonious balance of energetic resonances.

The activation of the Feminine Signature is an invitation for you to allow your deepest nature.

Archetypal Persona The Nurturer

The Nurturer knows the power of holding space, for themselves and others, to be seen, heard and known. The ability to receive and allow from the deepest part of themselves is formidable in its power and compassion and yet it requires work to fully receive abundance in all its forms.

The Nurturer shifts the lead from ego guidance to the intuitive knowing of soul. Courage and conviction are required to follow a path which sits outside of the rationale of intellect. Once nurtured into fullness, empowered intuition augurs confident assuredness in all journeys - both internal and external - and to a harmony within, which knows peace as the ultimate centre of self.

Balance is needed to ensure the ability to nurture is not just one-way and altruistic; nurturing the self sustains and enables much more. The Nurturer needs to give themselves permission to feel everything.

Qualities Courage, Intuition, Receptivity

The Feminine requires you to find the courage to both allow and follow your intuitive guidance with complete confidence and total commitment, trusting that its intention will always support both your deepest essence and living life. In doing so, you gravitate toward allowing and expressing your deeper nature because there is freedom from the plague of (insignificant) worries which distract and disrupt.

Courage calls for you to stand in your essence as it emerges and honour its space and truth; allowing yourself to be seen for who you are within and recognising that power can be gentle rather than fierce.

Receptivity calls for mastery - both in receiving all of yourself and in allowing material abundance. It is easier to hold space for and nurture others - to give more than you receive - and yet the dynamic of balance within energy demands that where one gives, one must also receive.

If you can view receiving as necessary in order to enable you to give, hold space and nurture others, then you will find the balance you need.

Activations Empowered Intuition, Receptivity, Allowing

As both quality and activation, receptivity demands you hold space to receive all that you need within yourself or life. In receiving yourself, you are able to embody all that you are and commune with your divine nature and it is important that does not equate spiritual or intuitive gifts with lack.

Empowered intuition asks to be your leading voice rather than remain a whisper only you hear. When you give it authority, you move from head to heart centred; from doing and thinking to being and feeling - being in the body and embodying the qualities and activations so that you *are* them - fully.

Intuition opens doors that you knew were there but have not been quite ready to walk through; an instinctive knowing that you will need to meet your deepest, most vulnerable self is what you have to allow.

Within all aspects of the Feminine, a key ask is not what you can *do* but what will you *allow*? Will you allow your empowered intuition to lead? Will you allow yourself to receive all that you are? Understanding what you will and won't, and can or can't allow, and why, are aspects of its work.

Soul Prompt Embrace Courage to Find Freedom

Breaking free from limitations and boundaries requires courage and courage enables freedom. In embracing the courage to stand up for yourself, to lead with your intuitive wisdom, to ask for what you need and in embracing the courage to receive yourself at your deepest level, you find freedom of mind and freedom within life. Courage is also required to give yourself permission to feel, and to be liberated through that.

Whenever you feel caged, lost or unable to trust who you are, the Feminine asks you to stand in courage and to simply ask 'what would courage do right now?' That's your answer and your liberator.

Personal

Foundation Activation: The Feminine activates your deepest self, the most vulnerable and open aspect of who you are and requires that you stand with courage and compassion in that, recognising it as your sovereign self. Courage is required to enable that deeper, and often vulnerable, self to be seen, known and to lead.

Your power is in creating boundaries which enable space to hold, receive and nurture yourself and others and in realising that strength comes in many forms, including allowing yourself to feel your emotions deeply and without judgement or fear. Empowered intuition strengthens and emboldens through life, calling to lead; when you meet that with confidence, life will make sense and you find acceptance within that.

An ability to trust what you cannot see but which you know to be true requires no explanation; it is its own validation and will support your courage in saying "no", saying "yes" and expressing yourself more freely.

Life creates growth by challenging you to never allow life to limit your intuitive nature or close you down; to never be smaller than you know yourself to be. Intuition blends with empathy; aligning with causes which need a voice to support them is a natural skill and often your courage shows itself more fiercely and freely when it is directed away from yourself. Yet it is through being courageous on behalf of yourself that you embody your deepest nature and enable freedom.

Leading Activation: You are encouraged to build confidence in allowing your intuition to develop and lead yourself and your life. Releasing the conditioning of fear and expectations about how life should be clears the way to empower a greater trust in your intuitive guidance when it goes against the logic of a situation or circumstance.

If you knew you could not fail, what would your empowered intuition guide you to? This is the question you are answering with the Feminine leading activation.

Courage in following through and standing up for your own needs determines both how easily you allow your deepest nature and the willingness to stand in its vulnerability and power; two halves of the same coin.

Embodiment supports you in realising what is true for you versus what is conditioning and it provides a tool to open the body as a receptor for wisdom that you feel deeply and trust completely, yet you must allow what you feel to be freely felt to enable this. Trusting what you cannot see but which you know to be true are moments which act as catalysts for an immense deepening of self.

As both Foundation and Leading Activation: The Feminine calls you to stand fully in your power and realise that there is another way. You come home to yourself and recognise that everything truly is within you.

Success - personal or professional - comes through standing consistently and purposefully in your power, trusting yourself and recognising that your strength comes from an unshakeable trust in your deepest self, of which empowered intuition is the messenger and guide.

Generally, the ability to develop the discipline of holding space for yourself will enable all that is required in terms of self-awareness and self-allowing. Boundaries will be tested because your radiating power will trigger those less confident in their own sense of self, or less inclined to trust anything other than logic and reasoning.

Business

Foundation Activation: Your business has the capability to lead with a nurturing, safe energy which creates a space for people to be free to be themselves and to feel wanted, respected and heard. An internal culture of respect and being valued supports your business.

It lends itself marvellously to all areas of business related to therapy, empowerment, feminine leadership and healing, where it is essential for individuals to feel held, seen and heard with compassion, care and consideration and where they are confident to lead from that nurtured and nurturing space.

There can be a natural inclination to speak up or speak out, to do business in a different way, to support those in need and to create change in industries or professions which seem to have lost their sense of humanity, care and connectedness; bringing heart back into business.

Success comes from standing in gentle but determined power, refusing to conform to old ways of doing things, and being courageous in seeking to create the caring space which is needed within its industry or service.

Leading Activation: Your business is encouraged to ensure it is aligned with how it wants to be seen, known and heard within its profession; leading from the front with confidence and compassion, with the ability to nurture - both talent and people - and empower. Your business is heart-led and it needs to lead from that even as it seeks to stand alongside its peers.

Materiality for materiality's sake will not work; there has to be a greater need, an ability to be a force for good within what it does and how it does it. Nuance matters, and details matter - if something doesn't feel right, trust that and align with what does.

Courage with change, and courage with leading change within your industry, also calls. Standing up for what is right, rather than what is normal, and standing in its own integrity authorises and empowers belief in its mission and what it is striving to achieve. Finding the balance between doing business, and doing business in a heart-led space and way can challenge.

Annual

The Feminine calls you to retreat and allow time and space to know yourself more deeply; to reconnect with the core of who you are, outside of the roles you play within life, and to start to embody a greater level of trust within yourself.

Intuition rises to the fore to enable understanding and insight and to engender change so that you can stand more fully in the deepest aspect of yourself with confidence and gentle strength.

Being consistent with your personal, or devotional practices ensures trust within yourself and trust in allowing a greater scope and freedom for your innate intuitive guidance.

There is the possibility for change which starts from within you and which takes courage to bring forth - the courage to say "no" to some things, to say "yes" to others but more importantly, courage to express who you are, what you stand for and what you need. Boundaries are important here and maintaining them matters.

Greater courage and a stronger level of intuition and trust can enable a year of immense personal growth.

Business Perspective: A Feminine year requires your business to realign to its compassion and heart. Ensuring a culture of openness and support within your business will reinvigorate and re-motivate and can lead to a change of direction. Change should be led with intuition; if it feels right explore further, if it doesn't, pause and re-evaluate.

19

MASCULINE

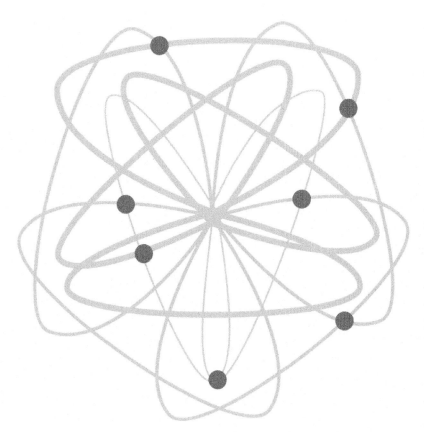

THE **MASCULINE** IS the discipline and structure which enables creative force and intuitive guidance to manifest through its form.

Within every aspect of soul is a logical process enabling the truth and energy of the soul to manifest its presence within and through life.

The activation of the Masculine Signature is an encouragement to take your potential forward within an appropriate structure.

Archetypal Persona The Authoritarian

The Authoritarian knows that strategy serves vision and creates the pathway to achieve it when actioned with consistency and discipline. Processes, systems and routines are aspects that come more naturally but can weigh heavily and there are times when greater spontaneity, and less responsibility, are desired.

The Masculine recognises that creativity requires a framework in which to explore and find its form. Trust can be difficult without a path to follow and there can be a reliance on the logical head rather than the centred heart; freeform is not their ideal way to move through life and whilst a practical approach and discipline create solid practices to enable progress, they can limit the potential for a more intuitive approach offering greater fulfilment.

When in doubt, the Authoritarian will revert to practicality and planning; an ideal is to have a strategy with solid systems and stepped approaches that can be relied upon, enabling freedom and fluidity within themselves.

Qualities Strategy, Discipline, Structure

A strategic approach, systematically actioned, spells achievement and success. The art of planning is a quality that supports so many aspects of life through its ability to create the path. The Masculine requires discipline to be implemented; whatever you want to achieve is a given with discipline in place. Without it, you can be muddling through the middle ground of progress without achievement, or taking longer and requiring more resources.

If strategy provides the plan and discipline, the approach is the third quality of the Masculine triangle (and yes, it would prefer a square!). Structure provides the framework within which the strategy is actioned.

Note: All of the Masculine qualities can be learned if they are not inherent within you and are the most straightforward of all the Signatures' qualities to master. By directly creating strategy, implementing discipline and enabling structure, you will be consciously activating the Masculine Signature and thereby empowering its energy to support what you are trying to manifest. Whether it is present in your profile or not, it is a Signature worth taking note of and choosing to work with when you need greater structure or more discipline to aid the journey to your goals.

Activations Logical Action, Disciplined Approach

Action provides a tangible outcome when it is done consistently. Without action, no matter what else may be in place, success in any area of life or business is rarely attained in the way one would like. This Signature creates the need for logical action. When activated, it impresses that logic determines the next step.

The approach taken toward any destination determines whether you reach it, how quickly and what it asks of you in terms of time, energy, money or anything else. A disciplined approach is the Masculine requirement and it will ensure that is the most direct, and successful, approach encouraging you time and again to master its art, no matter the goal.

Whilst discipline might not be the sexiest of activations, it will support you in all other areas of life. If you can master bringing a disciplined approach to your goals, dreams, aim and vision, there is nothing that you cannot achieve.

Soul Prompt Belief Encourages Success

A lack of belief - whether in your worth, ability or vision, is the one thing which can prevent you from working successfully with the Masculine Signature; belief encourages success, ergo if the belief was absolute, you would do the work to create the strategy and implement it. Your very belief would indeed enable its success purely through consistent action and a disciplined approach. You could not fail.

The Masculine establishes that if you don't implement the strategy, structure or discipline required, then you don't fully believe in, or desire, what you are trying to achieve or in your ability to attain it.

Personal

Foundation Activation: The attributes of structure, discipline and strategy are fundamental and returning to those when life challenges, whether personally or professionally, will always augur well. A structure which supports you generates freedom to experiment and explore because there are reliable systems, processes and routines underpinning you within life.

Although it can appear contrary, creativity is often innate within this; the more structure is in place, the more creativity is enabled because there is a framework within which it can find its form and become manifest. The more you embrace Masculine qualities and activations as a tool for creativity or growth, the more your potential expands.

The Masculine supports structure from a mindset perspective; harnessing its implicit energy supports the logical reframing of limiting mindsets or beliefs. Energy is always inherently organised - although it might appear random, it has structure, form and discipline. Within the Masculine activation, your energy is being mirrored universally by encouraging the organisation and shape of form.

Leading Activation: You are asked to employ strategy and structure to enable achievement. Leaning into structure, implementing systems and being consistent and disciplined is the route you need to take to reach your goals.

Strategy is something which can be learned; accept that you need to and that winging it will only get you so far. At some point, you have to be legitimate and create a proper plan of what you are doing with your life or where you want it to go.

This Signature suggests that leaving things to chance minimises the potential for success. It also challenges your belief, implying that if you don't do the work, you don't hold enough belief and would rather not try, than try and fail.

As both Foundation and Leading Activation: As the Authoritarian, there are no half measures - either you do implement and follow through, or you don't. Either you try or you *do*. Work with it rather than fight against it - and yourself - and it will support any aim you want to achieve.

Business

Foundation Activation: Your business thrives on strategy, systems and processes. They are its' lifeblood, enabling ease, growth and creativity, and effecting opportunity for your business to flourish because it is supported by solid foundations it can rely on.

Discipline and structure enable your business to know what it is aiming for and how it is getting there. This supports the clients your business serves by enabling it to meet its promise to them. It supports your team because each member knows their role, what they are doing, how they are valued and the contribution they bring.

Systems and processes of all sorts, from standard operating procedures to automation, enable a greater opportunity for growth and freedom as your business develops.

Strategy and structure can sometimes feel too solid and resist change, and yet all businesses have elements of change in them, particularly through growth. Allowing for adaptability within your strategy supports enabling the best of both worlds for your business.

Leading Activation: It is essential that your business adopts strategy. Whatever other qualities it has to offer, it will be more successful and sustainable by implementing a strategy with disciplined and consistent action.

Whilst a structure may seem restricting, your business's direction of travel will be smoother and quicker if you can embrace the need to have a clear and strategic plan.

Systems and processes take time initially, and yet these elements permit the back-end of your business to be supported more effectively, work more efficiently and free your time to work on your business or to allow the time or space you desire for creative or inspired insight.

You are asked to embrace your inner CEO and bring that to your business to ensure it leads with growth and has to tools in place to support that growth when it occurs.

Note: As with the personal activation, an inability to embrace the qualities and activations of this Signature imply that either you don't have the level of certainty you would like within your business's potential for success, or that you are not sure what direction you actually want your business to develop in. Either way, you are encouraged to master this Signature's ask because in not doing so, you may undermine the ability to succeed. In terms of systems and processes, if the Masculine Signature is a challenge for you, these are the aspects to outsource first.

Annual

There is a need to look at your achievements for the year through the lens of discipline. Whether personal or professional, you have more chance of achieving your goals if you implement strategy, enable structure and approach what you do with discipline.

Planning, reflecting, evaluating, adapting. All of these come into play within a Masculine year. Particularly with growth, this year is important because it is usually followed by the Emergence year. It can be more challenging to implement the growth offered within an Emergence year if the groundwork has not been properly set within the Masculine year - you would not expect to have a lush harvest if you had not ploughed the field, and done the preparation work necessary for your crop to flourish when planted. Have a plan for what you want to achieve and then execute that plan with a consistent, disciplined approach and you should end the year with your goals in line and coming to fruition.

Business Perspective: Look at strategy, structure, systems, processes and automation. These will enable a greater level of flow and freedom and they will directly support your business being able to develop and grow with greater ease. Don't be afraid of digging deep into planning and processes; teams can also grow this year and structure will also support onboarding.

20

EMERGENCE

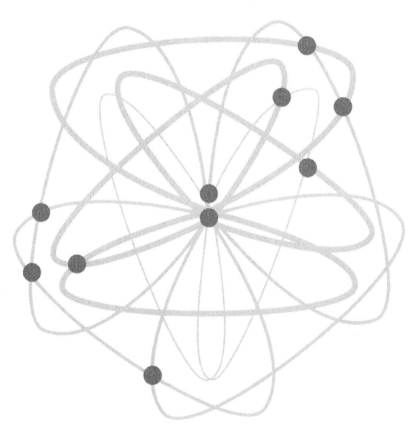

EMERGENCE IS the growth which enables the boldest, most sacred vision, and the certainty that if it can be envisioned, it can be attained.

Within every aspect of soul comes a moment where the emerging light creates a resistance which enables entrenched patterns of limitation to be released.

The activation of the Emergence Signature is an invitation to embrace walking the path which offers the greatest growth.

Archetypal Persona The Visionary

The Visionary has an innate ability to hold a vision with such clarity and dedication that it becomes real within before it manifests externally, the essential component of visioning.

Emergence imparts a propensity for growth over ease, taking risks over remaining with the familiar, and living for the adventure of life. A passion for growth in all areas of life supports the growth-mindset state, which directly generates the ability to be bolder, bringing a greater vision and potential into being.

The Visionary must remember that it is the journey as well as the vision which matters, for the vision can change as new potential and awareness emerges.

Qualities Vision, Growth Mindset, Risk Taking

Vision is the unconscious driver which develops to be a conscious dynamic. The ability to hold a bold vision, to feel it deeply and know it is attainable is a power that overrides any lack of skills or aptitude. All can be learned and the vision creates the dynamic energy, vitality and motivation to do what needs to be done in order to achieve it.

Emergence dictates the pathway of greatest growth because by meeting this, skills, courage and conviction are developed which enable a vision to be met. Developing a growth mindset is an essential quality; the lens which you choose to view life and its challenges through will directly impact how your goal is attained. Being able to master a growth mindset is the ideal which Emergence asks you to embody.

The Visionary does not generally lack self-belief; taking risks can be a natural ability or one you learn to be confident with. The more you lean into the vision and the certainty that you can master anything as you travel the path, the more confidence you gain in risk-taking, which is intuitively, as well as intellectually, guided. There is an instinctive knowing that risks are required to achieve the excellence which attains the vision, though it still takes courage and faith to take them.

Activations Adventure, Growth, Passionate Direction

Emergence activates the adventurer within who desires to be experiential and experience life fully. Spontaneity and the inclination to be adventurous - within life or through travel - directly lead to the capability to hold a wondrous vision.

Growth is always present. A desire to push through your own boundaries and see just what is possible when you liberate yourself from current limitations portends directly to growth, a steady companion which stretches you on all levels. The more you embrace growth, the more you realise how much growth still calls to be met. Standing still is not an option; a lack of growth can lead to lethargy, which drains vitality, drive and physical energy.

Feeling something so deeply that you know it to be true is what inspires the vision. A passionate desire for life to be fulfilling and purposeful drives motivation and the ability to bring a vision into being through the sheer force of your nature. The meandering road, though sometimes appealing for its comfort, is not a passionately aligned direction which summons purpose and potential.

Soul Prompt Courage Neutralises Self-Sabotage

Emergence, through its energy, calls for a boldness of vision which can only be met through courageously meeting your own limitations and liberating yourself from those patterns of behaviour which undermine your potential.

Whether through emotions or intellect, this Signature calls you to consistent, yet often unconscious, self-development work through simply being courageous enough to face a fear in the moment and power through.

Emergence's promise is that if you do this often enough, you will simply neutralise self-sabotaging behaviours as they occur.

Personal

Foundation Activation: Vision calls. Whether small or fantastic, there is the natural ability to envision a different life, a wilder possibility and to hold that energy with consistency. Vision creates purpose and momentum, without which, there can be a lack of energy, motivation or commitment.

Striving for something sparks passion within you, generating a capacity to reach for something expansive, creating a sense of adventure and stimulating the mind and emotions. If you can see it, you can believe it; if you can believe it, you can attain it, is the Emergence mantra.

Emergence leads with growth and growth is directly enabled through meeting and moving through resistance and challenge. There will always be times when a desire for life to be easier calls, yet an innate ability to see how growth is enabled is a driver which rarely lets you settle for easy.

It can be important to recognise that striving for something creates a pathway to a greater potential rather than assuring the aim will be met; vision always expands and recognising this contributes to a realisation that changing direction for a different vision is not failure (as long as, of course, you are meeting your resistance with courage).

Courage is required to face life and yourself head-on. Meeting your own resistance because of growth means that you'll need to overcome sabotaging patterns and behaviours at each level. The underlying gift is that by allowing courage to neutralise self-sabotage, you clear the way for immense growth because you no longer stand in your own way.

Leading Activation: Emergence asks you to reach for more than you believe is possible, choose growth at every opportunity and create the vision for a life you truly want to live. How easy this is depends on your foundation activation and the qualities and challenges it brings.

Developing a growth mindset allows you to see the gift and learning you are being offered within life, directly disarming overwhelm and enabling opportunity and greater self-awareness, strength, resilience and resourcefulness.

Emergence encourages you to keep moving forward rather than remain stagnant or too comfortable. Energy always meets its own resistance and the mind can take hold in that space of comfort, creating lethargy and procrastination. Consciously seeking vitality, drive and a motivating passion propel you forward with more ease. Emergence asks you to take a punt on yourself, start taking risks to achieve what you want and know that in doing so you are actively creating the pathway to success and fulfilment.

As both Foundation and Leading Activations: Growth is simply who you are. The ability to reach for a bigger vision than you (or anyone around you) ever thought possible comes naturally with both activations. Challenges come through the need to overcome your own patterns of sabotage and from what others may see as impossible or improbable.

You were born to hold the boldest vision and to bring it to life through sheer dedication to growth, a force of will and a deep belief that you can master anything as you meet it.

Business

Foundation Activation: Your business will naturally evolve its vision over time to meet its own potential and in doing so, it will ask you to grow with it and to believe in the possibility of a new vision. Steeped in the ability to know its own limitations and move through them into new opportunity, your business will always seek growth.

It wants to be bold, lead by example and show what is possible through vision and dedication to that. Its commitment to growth over staying the same, or accepting stability and security over expansion and possibility, can challenge your views of stability and sustainability.

Vision requires commitment and conviction; disparity of focus and a lack of clarity about the next right step ensues without this. Confidence is led by conviction, enabling the ability to take measured risks. How you view challenge as your business's owner will determine whether it is an obstacle or an opportunity and can make the difference between meeting a vision or circling it.

The sheer capacity for vision that your business has means it is not afraid to change direction. As long as the vision is clear, there is potential and opportunity for it to be attained.

Leading Activation: Emergence encourages your business to reach beyond its original remit and hold a vision for what might be possible. There will always be a point where you are faced with the opportunity of (sometimes) radical change versus retaining current stability. In choosing the former, potential opens but it requires risk and commitment to the journey. Go in fully or not at all.

A business that grows is a business with vision, attainable through a clearly defined and passionate purpose. As such, it will demand visibility and will seek to lead the way. Seeing all challenge as growth, and actively seeking the learning, will enable your business to navigate its path more easily and stand peer to peer with greater confidence and certainty

Emergence always offers a 'reach', never a certainty. Growth is enabled through your business moving past its limitations and becoming a more self-aware entity with a natural sense of evolution. Finding the courage to neutralise the voice of the nay-sayer and believe in the potential being presented, no matter the growth asked to be undertaken, is the key to liberating the full opportunity of Emergence.

Annual

Emergence offers growth through meeting personal challenge head-on, and moving through limitations and negative patterns to hold a bigger, better, brighter vision. It then vitalises a growth pathway to support you in achieving it.

It is a year to work on growth mindset and reframe limiting beliefs which are preventing the aligned growth you know is possible for you. Emergence will ask you to take risks in order to grow, to bet on yourself and to have skin in the game so that the end result matters.

Emergence challenges you to hold more, trust more, believe more and be more; leaps of faith, deep self-trust and the ability to put everything you are into the mix all herald.

Without reaching for something amazing in this year, you can feel as though you have let opportunity slip by. In its most basic essence, Emergence asks you to live your passion with conviction and to make its achievement non-negotiable.

Business Perspective: Review your vision and go bigger! Essentially that is the message of an Emergence year. It is asking you to look at growth for your business and re-envision where you want it to go. There are possibilities beyond current planning so be open to taking things further and opening to more potential.

21

SURRENDER

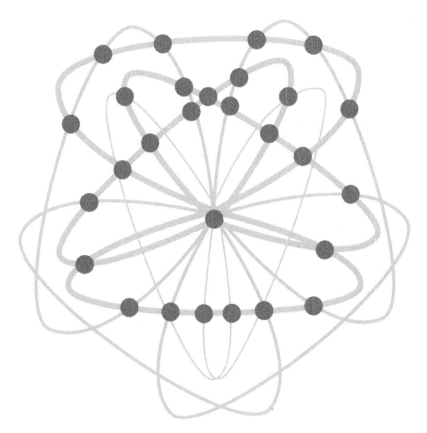

SURRENDER IS the deepest act of service to oneself and the divine potential within, activating self-belief through attainment of a greater purpose.

Within every aspect of soul we reach a union of energy where all parts of being and of life become guided by a greater intelligence.

The activation of the Surrender Signature asks you to surrender everything you are and have been to allow all that you can be.

Archetypal Persona The Humanitarian

The Humanitarian wants their life to matter, to make a difference where it counts, and this is attained through a deep connection and commitment to service.

Surrender imparts an instinctive understanding that life is not just a personal but a collective journey, as well as a collective responsibility. It can be difficult for the Humanitarian to detach themselves from the path of purpose; it must flow personally and professionally.

Self-awareness enables peace and a detachment from the drama and struggles which might otherwise detract. Yet within the surrender of self to fulfil a purpose, there is a need not to view one's own needs as being of lesser importance; in order to serve fully, the Humanitarian themselves must support, serve, nourish and sustain their own needs.

Qualities Collaboration, Service, Purpose

Collaboration leads these qualities, for a path of purpose cannot be walked alone. Collaboration is essential to fulfilling the service-aligned path in its entirety and this can provide challenges as there is a deep sense of self-containment and a preference to walk alone at times.

Service simply fulfils you, providing purpose and direction, and it leads to significant growth. Its call becomes stronger and its pull bolder as you move through life and as it begins to supersede individual purpose or desires. Whether you move to service earlier or later, all of life will have been preparing you and ensuring you are ready to meet it and fulfil it.

Direction and clarity of purpose serve you in understanding the reason you are called to this Earth at this time. Self-reflection can keep you centred in a circle of never-ending development, so being purposeful in deepening your aware-ness of yourself is essential for focused growth which drives, encourages, motivates and strengthens you.

Activations Self-Belief, Service, Unity

Surrender requires you to gain and master ever greater levels of self-belief in order to achieve all that you do. It impresses the need to not only believe deeply in who you are but powerfully in why you are here; this can determine the differ-ence between realising a life which you know makes a differ-ence or feeling as though you never quite meet the potential you know is within.

When in service to your purpose and to a divine purpose, you are you - fully and freely, deeply fulfilled, at your most powerful and your most influential. If you always lead from service, you will always be served. Finding the passion that resonates through you is the key and through it, you meet both a personal and higher calling.

Surrender recognises the wound of disconnection and separation as the cause of many of the world's ills and a recognition that unity within peoples, communities, social structures and cultures could enact incredible change. Unity, as a quality, serves two purposes with Surrender: unity within yourself through deep self-acceptance and a connection with your understanding of your divinity, and the unity which can unite behind a cause, for a purpose, around a concept or through a desire for change. Surrender asks you to embody unity within yourself and the ability to bring unity and to unify.

Soul Prompt Accept Divine Purpose

Surrender beseeches you to simply accept your divine purpose when it calls. It will not call at the time when you want or expect it to and it may take time to realise it has called! It won't be convenient or easy and it won't offer you the road you thought you wanted to walk.

In accepting it nonetheless, and committing to it with everything you are, you will find immense fulfilment and enable life in ways which bring extensive joy and empower a deeply grateful heart.

Personal

Foundation Activation: Serving fulfils you. A deep need to make a difference, in and outside of your personal life, is always present and if unfulfilled, it will create a space which always feels like it needs filling. In recognising that any space does not *need* filling, you create the dynamic for it to be filled from within; through that, you can find yourself, understand how you need to serve and ergo, your reason for being emerges.

Appreciating that everything you need is within you calls pause on seeking outside of yourself. Empowered belief becomes the path which opens channels of light so powerful that you cannot doubt your divine essence. In surrendering deeply, you discern surrender as a journey to light, albeit through shadow, authorising your power.

Returning to a desire to serve will always realign you to you, your values and to what you truly value within life when life takes you in different directions, requiring deeper levels of self-awareness and responsibility.

Humanity matters; kindness and helping people matter, necessitating boundaries and a deep level of self-care. Learning to serve yourself and be in service to your own needs empowers the sense of leadership required to serve a greater purpose successfully.

Leading Activation: Surrender asks you to seek the purpose which fulfils a greater desire or need than your own. This doesn't mean it shouldn't also serve you but it is a recognition that you will be served more fully if you serve a greater 'why'.

Life has taken you deeply into yourself, opening an awareness of more than the physical and requiring you to surrender to the path of self-acceptance, enabling freedom, encouraging growth and an exploration of what life has to offer. It is through experiencing life you meet the purpose within yourself, compelling you to want to be more and ensuring the knowledge that you are here for a more divinely-led purpose.

Purpose comes to you at the right time, in the right way, with a certain amount of challenge, for it needs to know your commitment. Whilst there may be different ways you seek to serve, ultimately, they will lead you to an overarching purpose; when you meet it you will realise life has been preparing you for it.

You meet yourself in purpose and service and it creates a unity within yourself where all parts of yourself come together as a divine whole which cannot be doubted. It is a moment of enlightenment, of absolute self-belief and the bringer of change as you move into accepting your divine purpose.

As both Foundation and Leading Activations: Your mission and purpose in life call beyond any personal desires and will lead you to a surrender of everything you thought you wanted, to fulfil an ultimate purpose. Whilst deep, personal fulfilment can be found with a double activation, personal sacrifice will play its part. You are serving your divine calling first; everything else falls behind that directive and in embracing that, you allow life to unfold for you with greater freedom and grace. Self-belief requires you to trust that all of your needs will be met.

Business

Foundation Activation: Surrender desires to ensure that your business seeks to serve a purpose greater than personal or material objectives. This does not mean it does not attain financial success, but the purpose must be more than money alone. When your business seeks to serve, it will achieve, grow and flourish because the energy reciprocity is assured: as it seeks to give and serve, so it shall receive back more than it gives.

Unity of purpose is important. The collective energy behind the business matters with this foundation activation; your team can greatly influence how your business develops, whether it thrives or whether it fights against itself and struggles to find the foothold it needs to flourish.

Ensuring that your business values are aligned with its directive, and that those values are mirrored in your team, support an aligned path which will create and open further opportunity as it serves.

This also sits with partners or collaborators - aligned values and intentions ensure success, achievement and service, so be discerning about collaborating as they must be invested in its purpose. Collaborating can enable your business to shift gears rapidly, offering expansion and opportunity.

Leading Activation: Surrender inspires your business to find a greater purpose. In doing so, it will centre and align around a stable foundation from which to extend and expand, enabling your business to flourish in marvellous ways. Purpose gives direction, supports motivation, encourages drive and innovation and it sparks inspiration because it seeks to serve and meet its best self in the process.

Collaboration and partnership play an important part, with collaboration a natural next step. No business is an island and a community or network working toward a common goal, united in a mission, creates a powerful flow of energy and enthusiasm which impacts and influences beyond that of an individual entity.

If you can find the purpose your business is here to serve, and a team which unites with passion behind it, it can impact globally, making an immeasurable difference. Surrender also seeks to achieve unity through its purpose and what that enables.

Surrender asks you to find the driver which you are passionate about (usually your life experiences will provide this) and bring it to life through aligning your business to it and holding the absolute self-belief that you were meant for this.

Annual

Surrender asks you to look at where you are and how you are living life; are you fulfilled, living on purpose, happy? Or are you simply going through the motions? Reflecting on your journey to date, and to considering what you would like to achieve or what you want your life to mean or stand for, are indicators. If it is not what you wanted or hoped for, Surrender invites you to make changes.

Internal change is often apparent with this Signature because it asks you to accept where you have been, who you have been and then move into something deeper. Surrender encourages you to do the work to clear outdated or limiting beliefs and to identify a deeper sense of purpose within yourself.

Surrender also suggests that it is never too late to make a difference and never too late to start something new as long as you are willing to commit to the journey. Live your passion and let that be the catalyst which opens the potential you are ready to step into.

Business Perspective: Surrender is a year where your business will benefit by looking at its purpose and really identifying how it wants to serve, what change it can engender within the world or how it can make what it does more meaningful and have a greater impact. It is also a great year for collaborating or partnering with others, as long as the purpose/vision aligns.

22

TRANSFORMATION

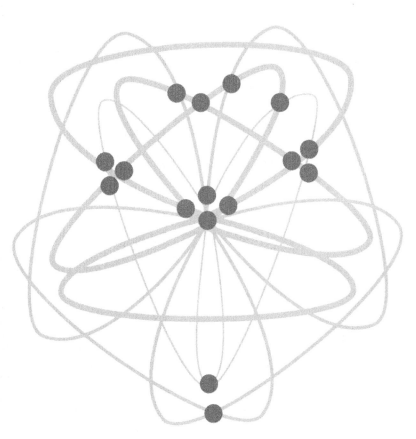

TRANSFORMATION IS the mirror of the self which alchemises shadow and light, instigating expansion and freedom from within.

Within every aspect of soul there is a balance between the light that we are and the darkness which enables the recognition of that which is the light.

The activation of the Transformation Signature is a movement into unconditional self-acceptance.

Archetypal Persona The Alchemist

The Alchemist seeks transformation through understanding and acceptance of the self at all levels, recognising the ability to transmute shadow into light and thereby discerning the potent power of shadow to transform. There is a need to implement and integrate the work rather than remain in a continual cycle of reflection.

Transformation supports the appreciation that balance maintains all aspects of life and authorises freedom from within to actualise through life, and when balanced aware-ness leads change, transformation occurs.

A deep ability to forgive releases burden; the ability to forgive oneself must also be grasped.

Qualities Balance, Freedom, Expansion

Balance leads transformation though requiring a mature approach to change. Alchemy transpires in the balancing of all elements and the compounding of step-by-step processes and small consistencies which, over time, enable deeper transformation than simple change - which often requires more luck than precision.

Freedom guides the longing for transformation; a need to escape restriction or boredom (from within oneself also) can lead to change without purpose - shifting the scenery temporarily yet ultimately returning one to the same place eventually, or creating circumstances which restrict further. It must be learned that freedom is always created within one's inner landscape first.

Expansion (of energy) is always present with Transformation; the longing to do more, be more and know more is felt deeply within as a realisation that there *is* more. The ability to cultivate the mind and unfold emotional intelligence is indicative of expansion in motion.

Activations Self-Acceptance, Forgiveness, Universal Love

Self-acceptance releases the necessity to flee from oneself and gifts the means to embrace oneself fully, creating freedom from within and liberating you from the need to change for change's sake. Supporting a simple acknowledgement of where one is within life creates the space to see the next steps with clarity rather than fear.

With the comprehension that internal freedom supports your ability to be freer within all areas of self and life, forgiveness provides the tool which liberates you from self-imposed restriction and it directly supports the awareness of love as both a personal and universal aspect, both within and without; a conscious energy you choose to intentionally inhabit and exhibit.

Soul Prompt Face Fear Through Trust

Transformation's prompt is for you to face any fear through trust; trust within yourself, trust in what's possible, trust in your resilience and fortitude (no significant change in self or life happens without it), trust in a greater sense of divine love and guidance supporting you.

Trust that you *can* rather than cannot.

Above all, Transformation says: when you face fear, where within yourself do you trust? Lead with that in the moment.

Personal

Foundation Activation: Transformation permeates your being with a desire for freedom, lending an ability to inhabit change in such a way it leaves a marked difference within yourself, life or your approach to it. Understanding what freedom actually means for you will enable change which actually creates transformation over time and it can be helpful to realise an underlying need of desiring to feel free within yourself.

Whilst the desire for freedom is the driver, the vehicle needs to be balanced change rather than change originating only through boredom, frustration, restriction or lack. A natural inclination for expansion - through physical or intellectual horizons - enables you to meet an intrinsic desire to be more and know more and can lead to a freedom of self even if life constricts in other ways.

Developing the ability to be consistent and follow through supports confidence and trust within yourself and in the decisions you make. Boredom and a need for variety can limit follow-through and thereby your ability to feel as though you can achieve.

Expanding your level of self-acceptance and the ability to forgive will enable you to meet yourself and life in the moment, lending clarity to the right next step and engendering trust within yourself and your ability to navigate your life in a way that works for you.

Leading Activation: Transformation encourages you to view and allow change as a natural process of transformative growth, expanding both your internal and external horizons, rather than as a restriction or inconvenience. You're meant to move into yourself as fully as possible, with as much acceptance as possible, engendering a sense of freedom and stability within yourself which then extends out into life.

Find balance to stabilise excesses and enable better levels of emotional intelligence, as strong emotions can trigger a desire to change something or anything; with more centre and objectivity they provide the insight to catalyse transformative growth. Understanding what freedom actually means for you will also support balancing a desire for instantaneous shifts with considered change.

If you can harness freedom from the inside out, then expansion will meet you there - bringing life and a greater energetic or cosmic awareness to you.

As both your Foundation and Leading Activation: It's essential to gain mastery over the need for freedom created through change and utilise change for lasting transformation; seeking the outcome of it, rather than seeking change itself, aligns you more fluidly with transformation and enables it.

A tendency to start but not complete limits potential and can be overcome. Recognising that transformation compounds over time and is in process before it can be seen, known and felt supports consistency, commitment, motivation and completion.

Business

BOTH Foundation and Leading Activations: Transformation suggests your business has the opportunity to transition significantly from its origins in order to meet growth and find its own way of navigating its path. Being aware of 'shiny object syndrome' ensures your business generates change that makes a difference.

It is not unusual for a Transformation business to change its focus, purpose, direction and path several times as it seeks to liberate itself from what it finds restraining or constrictive within its industry or profession. Expansion and growth are natural pursuits and they will bring your business into a greater sense of itself and extend beyond its current parameters.

Freedom does matter. The ability of the business to offer freedom to you or your team matters for its day-to-day aspects to run easily. Your business wants to enable a culture of freedom within it and it will seek to do that; culture, process, ideas or concepts, being valued and being heard all lend your business a sense of expansion - expansion of mind, of purpose, of possibilities.

Your business must know where it is going and what it is aiming for at any given time. Even within change, a clear vision and clear goal are essential so that your business doesn't veer off on tangents which do not serve its stability or longevity.

A Transformation activation wants to transform; it is its natural aim. It is the *how* of the transformation which matters.

Annual

This year brings a longing for more freedom and a sense of expansion within yourself, whether through learning, developing new skills, opening the mind, being more energy aware or any other way which enables a greater experience and an expanded awareness.

Freedom means different things to different people; your sense of what freedom means will either come into greater clarity (the penny will drop and you just know what enables it for you and what it means) or you will need to seek it. Deepening your levels of self-acceptance can provide clarity and can also help you move past (perceived) failures.

As with all aspects of the Transformation Signature, but particularly within the parameters of a specific time frame, i.e., a year, you are reminded that transformation is a change which transforms - either you, or life, or both. Try to enable change which matters rather than change for change's sake; being balanced and considered in your outlook and being objective about what is possible can support you.

Note: Whilst all Signatures can support and interact with each other, if you have significant Transformation Signature activations or influences within your profile, you'll benefit from activating the Masculine Signature if it isn't already present. The Masculine Signature can support the discipline and a framework within which the Transformation Signature can find form and balance.

Business Perspective: This year offers the opportunity to review how much freedom your business brings you and whether you are living the life you want to with your business. Expansion is possible but consider what it asks of you in return and ensure any growth is balanced and measured.

23

INTEGRATION

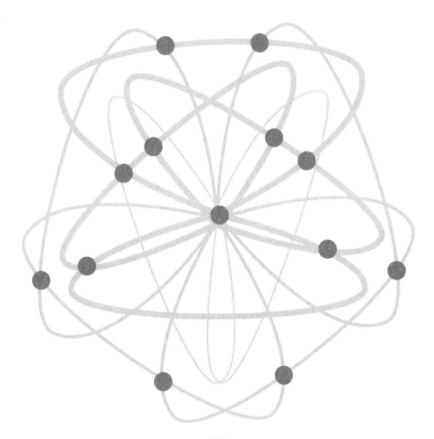

INTEGRATION EMPOWERS EVOLUTION and the natural ability to integrate change so that progression and forward movement occur.

Within every aspect of soul a moment is achieved where time simply becomes now.

The activation of the Integration Signature requires balance to a new paradigm within your energy; enabling adjustment to life, to yourself and to what is now required.

Archetypal Persona The Strategist

The Strategist has an innate ability to detach from self and see the bigger picture, integrating change from that perspective to define clear next steps for an aim to be met. When they know what action to take they can implement it with clear and certain knowledge the aim will be met.

Integration supports the idea that nothing ever stays the same, with change as life's most constant aspect, and supports a sense of liberation through the non-attachment to *what is* because the 'what is *now*' always evolves into something different.

Growth and change form parts of the Strategist's basic make-up and are generally balanced with a centred, grounded approach. Spontaneity may not be a natural aspect but it can be learned; the ability to be strategic needs to be humanised otherwise success which may not be fulfilling can be created.

Qualities Resourcefulness, Clarity, Evolution

Resourcefulness learned through experiencing life and all of its various circumstances stands you in good stead and imparts the certainty that you can find your way through any situation and achieve anything you set your mind to.

Natural objectivity enables clarity about what comes next and what is needed to support, or change, that. The ability to see clearly in the moment creates distance from emotionality or subjective constraints, and can be of significant benefit in creating the path you want to walk versus one you feel you have to tread.

A desire for life, and for quality in life, encourage natural evolution, reaching higher each time and for more (personal or professional) reward, with impartiality enabling what no longer fits the current time to be released.

Activations Liberation, Present Moment Awareness, Confidence

Liberation activates with the awareness that change is constant and only this moment is set, freeing you from unnecessary pressure or responsibility and gifting the objectivity to make decisions which aid the next right step at any given time, supporting the achievement of aims and aspirations.

Present moment awareness centres and grounds you, relieving oppressive emotions or worries and enabling a calm centre from which to move forward; freeing your energy and mind and creating a belief of the improbable being possible - because in the moment, everything feels achievable - inspiring confidence and insight.

The ability to see the larger plan, know how to work within that and implement, or integrate, what is required, brings confidence and inspires trust in your ability to navigate its demands. Confidence is also inspired by your ability to do the work and meet the needs of the moment with assurance and resourcefulness.

Soul Prompt Allow Change To Be A Friend

Integration encourages you to appreciate that each adventure is met by growth, enabling you to meet yourself and life with more depth, courage, confidence and belief. In allowing change to be a friend, you free yourself from a need for stability or security arising outside of yourself, for you recognise yourself as your stability and security.

Change is the companion which enables you to trust that confidence rises from within, with absolute certainty that no matter where or who you are within life, you are always evolving into more.

Personal

Foundation Activation: Integration supports meeting and integrating change with confident ease to enable progress and evolution. Comprehension that change and challenges within life are there to help you move forward, grow and evolve into a different stage of being or a different level within life, supports a sense of security within yourself, cultivating confidence and an aptitude to meet life where it is at.

An awareness of needing to move forward unencumbered by the past (baggage), and a willingness to do that, enables swifter progress but it must be tempered with humanity. It is easy to view things too objectively and close yourself off from the emotional resonance of life.

Objectivity in the moment upholds clarity and enables strategic thinking and decision-making; attaining goals directly equates to evolution whether on a spiritual, mental or emotional level or within life in general, allowing greater insight into yourself with each. Even as you have one foot in the next stage, the other is in mid-air, transitioning, and there is the ability to balance and integrate change in differing areas at the same time.

Being able to balance these different aspects of being, change and paradigms, to almost enable a consistently shifting 'whole' is a fundamental learning that Integration asks you to master, for it is this which creates the space of expanded potentiality where all is possible.

Leading Activation: Integration guides you to be aware of always 'being' whole, no matter how fractured you or life may appear or feel. Integrating changes - in life and within yourself - matters as your sense of stability and security impact how confidently you approach life and the risks you allow yourself to take.

It can be easy to lose a sense of yourself within all that is going on and feel comfortable staying there, disconnected from a greater sense of emotional connection and giving focus to a more intellectualised version of yourself; yet Integration requires you to realise that you are actually never lost and that, in the present moment, you have full cognition and amazing clarity.

Release and healing act as catalysts for evolving into a different state of being or awareness; there is a capacity to delve into your psyche and uncover causal issues which show themselves as separation within life or which hold your energy in past patterning rather than enabling the natural evolution of your energy, awareness and potential.

As both Foundation and Leading Activations: You are asked to consistently move forward and evolve into the next stage of life and being. Trust that you are not meant to remain where you are, nor meant to be comfortable or contained but rather to liberate your energy and your mind, enabling greater confidence to explore life, integrating learnings and experience to inform the next stage. Travelling light is required, for you cannot progress as desired carrying lots of baggage!

A roadmap which mixes the magic and timelessness of present moment awareness, where you simply *are,* and the ability, in those moments, to clearly see not just the direction ahead but also the plan of how to get there, are where Integration seeks to lead you. It liberates you from the narrower vision of a third-dimensional reality and opens an evolutionary path, not just in life but within your spirituality.

Business

Foundation Activation: Your business has the ability to integrate changes or shifts in industry, marketplace or itself with enviable ease. There is an aptitude to meet challenges which cause, for example, a change in focus or in the way one does business, in a way which enables your business to evolve to meet the needs of the moment, supporting its potential for longevity.

Your business wants to upgrade. It wants to move with the market. It wants to be in with the front runners and this is natural because Integration as the tenth Signature also has an underlying Initiation Signature activation.

Innovation and evolution go hand in hand. One innovates to evolve and evolving requires one to innovate. Your business's ability to stand the test of time is enhanced with Integration.

The more it stands firmly in the present - leaving behind past aspects which no longer support its vision and yet not looking so far ahead that it misses opportunities in the moment - the more confident it becomes and the more confidence it inspires.

Leading Activation: Integration encourages your business to evolve rather than try and stay the same for a sense of ease, stability or security. Learning to be confident with embracing change (for a purpose) is part of its path and within that, liberating practices, offers, programmes, institutions, team members etc., which limit or no longer integrate with a new sense of direction is necessary.

A lean business moves into change and a different way of being more easily. Be strategic in the path your business takes so that everything forms a cohesive whole.

Innovation is also present as a subconscious activation. The ability to be curious and open about how to stay current support this. Evolution is about change which opens a new level, so there will be a need to look at things differently and explore what works and how to make things work in a way which enables a sense of connectedness, and sustainability, throughout the business.

Generally, allowing your business to be brave and grow in confidence is also an aim with Integration; as the Signature of the Strategist, *be strategic rather than winging it.*

Annual

There is a need to spend time and energy integrating aspects of change which have occurred recently as this year calls to you step into the next level of yourself.

Clarity is present; you will see things in a way you haven't before, impressing a clearer direction and the steps or action which is required. Embrace change and take the action.

Trust that stability, security or reassurance can only be found within you and that you are being asked to find it.

The more you can be present, the greater clarity you'll have and greater confidence in that clarity. Be open to insight which guides you to awareness of energy - what is present within you and what needs healing, releasing or forgiving. Being present is what allows you to know what has been integrated and what requires further work.

This year can often provide recognition, and enlightenment, about your journey through recent years. Be confident! Allow it to enable more trust in your ability to navigate your path and in your resourcefulness.

Business Perspective: Integration encourages your business to follow the natural path of evolution. This may include reducing or releasing parts of it that no longer serve the vision, so that it feels aligned as a whole. There may be new paths or aspects that are innovative; explore and be curious about what may work. This is the next stage in growth, a level-up rather than simply change.

24

DEVOTION

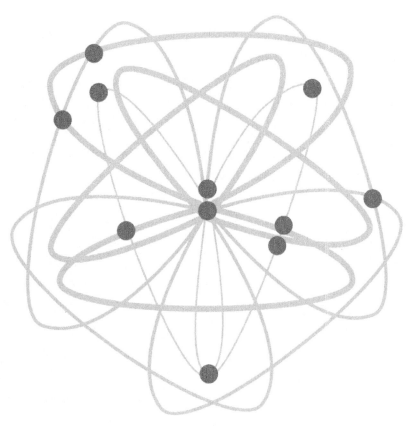

DEVOTION REALISES LEADERSHIP, attained through mastery and standing in integrity, empowering leading from soul.

Within every aspect of soul one moves to a point of mastery, a moment of infinite integration and accelerated activation; mastery of the soul within mastery of the being.

The activation of the Devotion Signature signals leadership through expression of the soul.

Archetypal Persona The Leader

The Leader doesn't always seek to lead, yet the call to lead will be inevitable. A sense of devotion to a cause (and that cause can also be personal or to soul) seeks its purpose through you; ergo, the call is answered.

Devotion requires excellence, gaining mastery over oneself and over aspects and skills within life; being accountable, responsible and driving their car rather than being the passenger in it.

A natural ability to lead by example, even in the smallest of ways, supports integrity and directly enables aspiration to personal or professional mastery, or both; it becomes essential that they act in accordance with their words and beliefs.

The Leader brings all aspects of themselves into a known whole, with a self-awareness that disregards the need for perfection, recognising that one's best, in any moment, is the continual progress which needs to be met.

Qualities Leadership, Mastery, Integrity

Leadership is a quality which develops as you move through life; something that you naturally step into, sometimes by default or sometimes through recognition of it as a calling. Devotion recognises leadership as the ability to empower and enable others as well as lead oneself within life.

Challenges inspire mastery - within the self (on all levels - mindset, emotional intelligence, energy) and within life or business (skills, ability etc.) The ability to commit and master what you need to directly supports your ability to step into leadership. As you continually learn and lean into your own mastery, so you naturally lead more and are seen as a leader.

Standing in your truth and acting in accordance with that matters. Being out of integrity can cause you to stagnate and halt progress because you feel yourself to be less than you know you can be. Integrity is the foundation stone which enables leadership and mastery.

Activations Unity Consciousness, Divine Expression, Grace

There is a level within Devotion which can only be met by recognising your role in a bigger (universal) picture (either actively or subconsciously) - whether you see that spiritually, universally or simply within the bigger picture of life and the world. What you do and how you do it matters; you know this and it guides you to stand in integrity and lead from that.

Divine expression is activated as you're called to express your divinity, your core essence and full energy, through more than your words. It is expressed through your deeds, actions and how you live your life. You bring all of yourself to the table, able to recognise limitations, accept them or move through them, and balance is enabled where ego is supported rather than leading.

The ability to know oneself deeply and allow yourself fully, without apology and yet with humility, activates Grace and the knowing of your own divine nature, irrespective of any religious connotations, which simply allows your essence to flow.

Soul Prompt Embrace the Process of Life

Devotion encourages you to ride the wave of life and to let it carry you to destinations you could not have envisioned for yourself. There will always be visions you hold, aims and desires you wish to achieve, and these provide a roadmap for your journey.

Yet there will be detours and diversions; embrace these as the process of life, trusting that it is always working for you, knowing that within each detour there is learning which supports and serves you for your good, growth and happiness.

Personal

Foundation Activation: Devotion requires you to stand in and lead from integrity, allowing your actions to match your words and leading from that. It is a quality that runs through you and allows you to align with truth. What you do and how you do it matters hugely; the quick fix only works temporarily.

Challenges arise for specific moments where you have to pull everything you are out of the bag to get through, teaching you to be the driver of your own car rather than the passenger and ensuring you can drive your car on any terrain, under any conditions.

A practice which centres and supports a connection to self is encouraged, cultivating awareness of where you need to gain mastery over aspects of yourself. You gain the understanding that there is no wrong or right; there are simply patterns of behaviour, mindset or emotion which you can change to allow an aligned, balanced and empowered self to be more present, more often.

The need to do things properly and well supports diligence, confidence and the ability to master what you put your mind to.

Devotion encourages the sound and certain knowledge of who you are, authorising your ability to stand in your full energy, with compassion, strength and kindness, leading from soul rather than needing to feed the ego. Natural leadership emerges.

Leading Activation: Devotion asks you to look at where you are leading your life and where you are being led, because it encourages you to stand more fully in your own energy and lead who you are, completely.

Its challenge is to encourage you to gain mastery over yourself, a pattern present through life; situations where you have been asked to master your emotions, take control of your thoughts, believe in your ability and capacity to learn new things totally outside of your comfort zone at that moment in time. This empowers your ability to lead and inspires your confidence in navigating change.

There is an awareness of spirituality, of a divine or greater connectedness and Devotion asks you to ground that heightened awareness through practical application so that you can live it within life, being in integrity with all of your beliefs and allowing actions, deeds and expression to be led by this.

A rooted, solid practice that always takes you back to yourself will support you in seeing and knowing the bigger picture when the ask of life seems too big.

As both Foundation and Leading Activations: Everything is about finding the leader within and allowing that to find its purpose and expression through life. Leading from integrity is essential and the more you can master yourself, the more you will expand into the purpose and expression life opens for you.

Business

Foundation Activation: Devotion supports your business to be a leader in its field or industry; it wants to lead, excel and often create change in how its profession or industry is seen.

It will call for courage and steadfast confidence from you and it is essential that your business stands in integrity; it needs to act in accordance with its promise and fulfil its offering to the letter.

Striving for excellence means that it will challenge the attitude and status quo around it; things don't evolve and reach new standards by standing still. It needs to have the courage of its convictions. Openness, honesty and full transparency will always support it.

Leading Activation: Devotion encourages your business to step outside its current comfort zone and seek to be a leader within its industry. No matter how stable or consistent your business is, Devotion impresses that it has the potential to be an architect of change and to create, or create greater, integrity and an attitude of leadership in its area of expertise.

Whatever doesn't align with your business currently - services or different ways it diversifies - you are being called to bring things together so that your business can stand in its full power with honesty and certainty, to enable it to move forward with full integrity.

Your business seeks to serve a purpose. It is called to that through leading its field and standing for excellence and mastery in what it does and how it does it. If you knew it could not fail, where would your vision for it lead?

As Devotion is the eleventh Signature, it also aligns with Resonance as an underlying influence. If your business can always come back to aligning with its truth and being in flow with its values, it will consistently meet its purpose and expand through and beyond that to the excellence it seeks to stand for.

Annual

Devotion asks you to find the leader within, trust it and create a culture of leadership within your being and your life. Where are you being led rather than leading? This needs to change, for it isn't serving you or your purpose.

Mastery is essential. Where you do let yourself down or self-sabotage? How can you work to master these patterns so that they no longer derail you? Where don't you honour the promises you make to yourself?

Devotion also calls you to know yourself more deeply and to allow more of yourself to be seen; it encourages a devoted practice to enable this. Whether through meditation or something else, a connection to your inner stillness and divine power is the way for personal awareness and sustained self-reflection, which makes a difference.

As Devotion is the eleventh Signature, it calls to a sense of closure. In readiness for a new chapter, you are encouraged to prepare by working to eradicate behaviours which negate your ability to succeed and lead in the way life calls you to.

Life rarely goes to plan; the process of life has enabled you to learn and embrace skills, awarenesses and strengths that you otherwise might not have realised. Whichever avenue opens up next, embrace the process by stepping in and leading yourself in all areas of being.

Business Perspective: Devotion is a year to lead, for your business to step up, to take its place as (more of) a leader in its field, to strive for excellence and to know that it can deliver at that level. Let it stand in its truth and own what it does, how it does it and, most importantly, why it does it that way, and opportunity will arise.

If in Doubt, Choose Simplicity

Before we move further and look at case studies so that you have an idea of how to bring the individual Soul Signatures within your profile together as a whole, I'd like to suggest to you that soul can be as complex or as simple as you want it to be.

You can delve *deeply* into each Signature, using the information given in Part Two to guide and encourage your own instinctive interpretation of them, pulling out complexities or nuances which enable greater depth of understanding (and work), or you can work with them as simply as possible by asking yourself straight-forward questions relating to each of the Signatures, such as those detailed below.

As all Soul Signatures are within your energy, by asking the simple question and responding to it, you are working with that Signature and actively permitting its support.

I would invite you to use freeform journaling, asking the question and then allowing yourself to just write freely and flowingly in response with no judgement or expectation, and no editing. The next step or the answer you need will be in your words.

Initiation

Where do I need to innovate and trust that I can do things differently?

Resonance

Where do I need to align my energy, and what work should that take, to enable flow?

Commitment

Where do I need to honour and express my truth?

Anchor

What reinvention is calling and how can I honour and bring forward into life the change I feel within me?

Feminine

How can I nurture myself and my energy to enable my intuition more directly and with greater clarity?

Masculine

Where do I need to be more disciplined and enable strategy or structure to lead?

Emergence

What is trying to emerge in my life to enable my greater light or show me where my growth path is?

Surrender

Where do I need to surrender control and allow my divine purpose to come further into being?

Transformation

Where do I need to stop trying to change and actually step into transformation?

Integration

What aspects of life, or myself, require integration to allow alignment and a sense of wholeness or purpose?

Devotion

Where do I need to lead more in myself or my life and what do I need to master to enable this?

PART III
CASE STUDIES

25

CASE STUDIES

IN THE CASE studies I've shared, you'll find short key points for each activation and influence with a fuller summary. I've shared them this way to enable you to see how the Signatures come together as a whole, giving a broader view of how the qualities of soul are influencing. I've included their main annual Signature influences, the Signature which is active for the majority of their year.

26

CASE STUDY ONE - 'AMY'

AMY HAD a Soul Signatures for Business Profile so we were looking at the four key Signatures supporting her business. Amy is a leadership coach.

Foundation Activation: Commitment
Leading Activation: Transformation
Inner Influence: Commitment
External Influence: Emergence (Secondary: Anchor)
Annual: Resonance

<u>Foundation Activation</u>: Commitment supports truth and courageous expression. The business can't be something that it isn't as it will not align with the energy supporting it. Its stability and growth can be more challenging without this alignment.

<u>Leading Activation</u>: Development within business occurs because there is a need for freedom and expansion. Both Amy and her business learn and grow from each other and changes in one are reflected in the other. Patience and balance will help to navigate changes, supporting insight to enable transformation rather than simply change.

<u>Inner Influence</u>: The Commitment Signature is the soul quality that Amy brings to her business and it speaks directly to the need and desire to stand in and express truth. This empowers her business's own foundation activation: truth is essential.

With Commitment, Amy will also be asked to walk her talk and to be authentic in what she does and how she brings that to her business.

<u>External Influence</u>: Emergence empowers the business to develop a greater vision and be willing to take risks in order to accomplish all that is possible for it - taking the road of greatest growth to fulfil a greater potential.

<u>Annual</u>: Resonance brings qualities of Aligned Energy, Belief and Flow indicating a need to align different areas of the business and bring them together as a cohesive whole.

How her business flows and how it aligns to and with its value are all supported by the Resonance Signature and will influence the emerging understanding of a greater truth - what it is really here to express and how it does that.

Where Amy feels limitations with her business, or within herself within the business, this year supports the subconscious work undertaken to shift them; making the effort will make a difference.

Summary: As her business is led by the Transformation Signature, it supports the ability to transform the business to stand fully in truth and to align with Amy's truth as an individual. Transformation also presents the need for those things that do not align to be removed in order to create the opportunity for the next step and the next stage in her business's growth.

With Commitment as its foundation, it will seek out its own truth, leading to changes within what it does and how it does it. This will be guided by Amy as Commitment is her birth Signature, ensuring truth and aligning with truth, as essential for all that she does, both in life and business. It will be difficult to enable a business which does not align with Amy's values. Commitment is heavily aspected as it relates to her first name also. Standing in truth matters.

Emergence assures a growing desire to make a mark with the business and to make it in a big way. Commitment suggests that when Amy and her business are fully aligned, she will want that truth to be heard and her business to find its own voice, to stand out from the crowd and have its own space at the table. This is reinforced by a secondary external influence of Anchor, supporting the business's ability to reinvent itself to meet its needs. Anchor also creates the ability to embed change and a desire to always move forward, which can be a challenge in letting go of elements which work or which are successful but which don't align with a newer vision.

A *personal* external influence of Surrender brings the desire to be of service. It's a quality Amy should be able to recognise as coming more into being. This lends itself to the work that she does, her truth needing to be used, expressed and given in a way that serves and enables others.

Finally, there is a notable absence of the Masculine Signature within the business profile, which relates to systems, processes and structure. It may take more work to get systems and processes in place as that naturally logical energy is not as present within relatively creative energy. Working on enabling a greater level of Masculine qualities will support change within the business, or it can be outsourced, but it should be a consideration.

27

CASE STUDY TWO - 'BELINDA'

BELINDA'S PROFILE is also a business profile. She is a Medium and Tutor but unlike 'Amy', Belinda's own name forms part of her business name so we also reviewed the Signatures relating to individual names.

Foundation Activation:	Feminine
Leading Activation:	Commitment
Inner Influence:	Resonance
External Influence:	Feminine (Emergence, Anchor & Devotion support through individual (personal) names which are in the business name)
Annual:	Surrender

Foundation Activation: A foundation activation of the Feminine brings the business back to its need to serve and nurture, following the path of the greatest good and holding space for that. Courage in allowing intuition to lead is required. It is present and will strengthen through time.

Leading Activation: Commitment asks Belinda to stand in and commit to truth; the truth of what she believes in and of what she wants her business to stand up for. As commitment activates courageous expression, it will support clarity of message and purpose.

Inner Influence: Resonance is the consistent energy Belinda brings to her business and it is totally about energy - flow is important and an awareness of energetics supports both her and her business. Momentum is important; periods of significant growth and the belief that Belinda brings to business (and the impact it makes) is the anchor which enables it to make the most of momentum and reap its benefit and growth. Solid belief creates flow.

External Influence: The Feminine qualities align and empower the foundation activation, encouraging and strengthening empowered intuition as part of the business. There is a strong altruistic aspect here but it needs to be balanced with an awareness of allowing her business and herself to receive in abundance and with gratitude.

Annual: The annual Signature is Surrender which supports an identification with a deeper purpose and the acknowledgement that above all else, Belinda's business needs to be of service.

Collaboration lends strength - whether through development and learning, which opens up potential and new ideas within oneself or with partnering professionally or energetically.

With this is also the recognition of the business as a business and a commitment to its path in that respect. It activates self-belief and unity so she will be challenged to truly bring all aspects of her work and business together and to really believe in what she does and within herself as part of that.

2022 brought a year where aspects of the business may step back; where they don't align or where they don't fall into the vision of its purpose moving forward, Belinda will be encouraged, through greater awareness of purpose and service, to prune and to step back from personal desires to enable a path with greater impact.

Additionally, 2023 brings a Transformation Signature. This is about change with qualities of Balance, Freedom and Expansion and so, changes that are instigated this year will come to a clearer fruition and power in 2023. Belinda is urged to balance change however, to ensure the freedom and expansion the business seeks is sustainable.

Summary: Belinda's business name is an interesting mix of determined and soft, receptive energy.

With Commitment and Emergence, there is an inherent strength and truth which is determined, forthright and seeks to make an impact bringing a vision and purpose to life. This is tempered by the desire to serve and to make a difference in the world.

The softer energy of the Feminine enables compassion and empathy as a clear aspect of the business with 'Belinda' (Emergence) lending strength and determination; Anchor, through middle and last names, supports the ability to persist, move with change and come through the other side with greater strength and resilience.

Emergence empowers the natural courage and resilience that Belinda grows into throughout life; it embeds within her the ability to take the path which offers adventure rather than choosing the easier, simpler route. As she moves through life, the direction she is travelling and wishes to travel unfolds, becoming clearer. This clarity lends confidence in steering her ship and within the decisions she makes.

Belief is essential to really enable the business to flourish and with the correlation of the Feminine as both the foundation Signature and personal Signature, belief within the business comes from a belief in self which is empowered, and which grows through personal courage and a deeply intuitive understanding of the self and a commitment to walk that path.

'Belinda's' last name offers a Devotion Signature, signifying Leadership, Mastery and Integrity. It is a significant Signature as it is very present in her current, used name. A deep desire to master her craft and bring leadership to what she does subconsciously encourages her to leadership in her field; even if other Signatures suggest a 'play down' of this role it will rise more strongly and with greater determination over time.

As long as Belinda's business aligns through truth and she feels aligned to it (and to what she does), this will translate to strength and a deep commitment to truth within her business, enabling aspects of thought leadership and encouraging real accomplishments in the field of its industry.

2022 offered the opportunity to really consider what service and purpose mean and how she wants to bring that to the world, with 2023 offering the opportunity of transformation to enable this.

28

CASE STUDY THREE - 'CONSTANCE'

CONSTANCE'S IS a personal Soul Signatures Profile, so we were looking at all Signatures from a personal perspective.

Foundation Activation:	Masculine
Leading Activation:	Devotion
Inner Influence:	Feminine
External Influence:	Anchor
Annual:	Anchor

Foundation Activation: The Masculine Signature ensures that process and structure will support Constance. The Masculine activates logical action and a disciplined approach so there will always be the need to balance the energetic aspect of Devotion with practicality within life. Remember that the masculine processes are there to support rather than to constrain.

Freedom is created within a framework in which it finds its form, so allow the discipline and structure of this Signature to provide the stability within which creative expression is able to find a powerful form to express itself within life.

Leading Activation: Devotion is the Signature of the Leader and it calls her to mastery within life and being. Activating unity consciousness and divine expression enable Constance to meet and know herself through her divinity, requiring her to bring that aspect of herself to life. Devoted practice will always support her because it brings her back to her centre.

Inner Influence: The Feminine relates to the most used name, 'Constance', bringing the ability to create and hold space, for herself and others, and asking Constance to allow her deepest nature - a true connection to her core essence. In doing so, empowered intuition is enabled, which grows stronger through life as it seeks to enable her to lead with it. Courage is always an ask with the Feminine Signature. It will ask her to stand up for who she is, what she believes in and what she needs. Placing boundaries and enabling self-care are also key indicators of this Signature.

External Influence: Anchor resonates with Constance's current full name and it lends itself to the ability to reinvent herself through significant change. The ability to be creative with surviving change, and indeed, having to be, are indicated here and with Devotion, a connection to a centred sense of the divine sustains, supports and enables her to meet reinvention with courage and determination.

Anchor asks Constance not to get too comfortable with where she is or too settled. Its nature is reinvention and when the need occurs, its activation will present strongly, whether in life situations or circumstances or personally.

Annual: Anchor is also her annual Signature and it calls Constance to honour her path and recognise the aspects of change calling now. As it relates to shedding who she no longer is, there will be calls to release aspects of identity or attachment to an identity that are no longer relevant.

Shedding habits or routines that no longer serve a purpose can be made with greater ease.

Stepping into more than Constance believes she could previously is a change which challenges her personally - where can she meet what calls within and bring it into her life?

She needs to be creative with any change which is brought to her rather than sought and be honest about why she is resisting personal change within herself. If it is calling, it is calling for a purpose and in order to meet that purpose, Constance has to be prepared.

Whilst she may want to relax into ease or a more comfortable or complacent period, Anchor always calls for forward movement.

Summary: Overall, this is a balanced profile with a solid foundation in the Masculine Signature, supported by Constance's personal influence of the Feminine. Natural intuition is supported by process and she not only allows it but also understands it. The foundations provided by the Masculine Signature enable her to reach further - think about deep roots enabling extension and expansion - and this directly supports the Devotion Signature which leads her.

Therefore leadership and mastery are ably supported and Constance will find that leadership calls in all areas of life. She does have to be the driver of her car; being a passenger is not an option. She is able to meet the masculine demands of life with the soft strength of the feminine and enable the compassionate courage of the feminine through the authority of the balanced masculine.

The ability to meet the ask of the Devotion Signature is empowered by Anchor. Change takes Constance further into herself enabling more of herself to be present within life. The leader within steps forward and starts to lead with authority and with a recognition that there are accomplish-ments she can, and will, achieve that she would not have believed previously.

The ability to master herself supports all of Constance's Signatures and their activations. Whether through mindset, emotions or in life, mastery is supported by the discipline of her foundation activation; the discipline which enables her to get on with doing the work.

PART IV

WORKING WITH THE SIGNATURES

29

WORKING WITH THE SIGNATURES

I WOULD LIKE to begin Part Four of Being Soul Confident by reinforcing that the Signatures within your profile are already very present. They are the more generally impactful energy of soul and you don't need to activate or work with them specifically unless you want to embody their values in a deeper way, enabling their fuller authority, or for a specific purpose.

Simply by identifying your Signatures and reading about them in this book, I hope you will have gained a sense of clarity and reassurance about how soul *is* influencing you - guiding you through growth and expansion - supporting you in being more confident in allowing yourself more fully, trusting that in doing that, you *are* leading from soul, standing in the sovereignty of yourself and being soul confident.

Yet within humanity, deeper self-awareness, greater commitment to self and personal development and a desire to be all that we can be are aspects which are very present and becoming more so. As human beings, we are evolving to know ourselves more fully and allow ourselves more consciously. Choosing to actively facilitate leaning further into that divine essence cultivates a more tangible experience of soul, imbuing the potential for more confidence in allowing it to lead and an understanding of its finer nuances and impulses. When you choose to lean in, you are giving soul permission to support you more fully.

What you focus your attention on expands; focusing your attention on soul enables it to expand and work more of its magic with you and for you, so I'd like to share some practical and energetic ways to work with the Signatures, and invite you to align more deeply with your potent essence, permitting its greater impact within you and your life, and supporting you to navigate the path to fuller potential, deeper fulfilment and more joy, with greater ease.

I believe that when you are able to understand something and work with it in relatable and practical ways, you enable it. Your mind accepts it, it starts to make sense and you use it.

Soul is inherently energetic; it would be remiss of me not to include ways that you can work with the Signatures in a more energetic capacity, should you so wish.

30

HOW TO DETERMINE WHICH
SIGNATURE TO ACTIVATE

IF YOU ARE anything like me, you will have read the information for all eleven Signatures, and whilst your attention may have been more focused on those within your Soul Signatures Profile, there will be other Signatures that you want to align with because their qualities, activations and soul prompts will either benefit you or you think they simply rock!

You *have all eleven Signatures* present within the energy of soul so you can choose to activate *any* Signature, at *any* time. (I'll caveat that by impressing upon you that you will be required to do the work of the Signature!)

Working with Signatures within your profile will enhance, stimulate and activate them further and they can be a natural choice and a good way to start directly working with the Soul Signatures. Whether you want to enhance their activation or activate a different Signature, I would always invite you to consider the same question:

What do you *need* at this moment in time?

I use the word **need** deliberately as soul serves need rather than want.

Base your Signature activation on what you *need*. For instance:

- If you are feeling as though life is relentless, that you are constantly under pressure, feeling overwhelmed and with no time for yourself then I invite you to consider activating the Feminine Signature.
- If you're struggling with people pleasing and you need to express who you are, follow your path and your truth, a Commitment activation will support this.
- If you feel the lure of huge growth, you know you've done so much development work but you keep going around in circles with nothing actually moving, activate either the Initiation Signature (encouraging you to view things differently and to innovate to open opportunity) or the Integration Signature (to ensure growth has been integrated and you are ready for the next step).

It can be useful to consider the balance of energy within your Soul Signatures profile. If you have a Masculine Signature which appears more than once in your profile and no Feminine or Surrender Signature, it can support you to activate one of those as they'll alchemise a finer balance within you generally.

31

PRACTICAL ALIGNMENT WITH SOUL SIGNATURES

WE'RE GOING to focus on qualities, activations and soul prompts as these as the relatable, tangible aspects. They are all asks of soul in differing ways and, ideally, you want to embody the qualities and activations as fully and consistently as you can. It can be helpful to think of them like this:

Qualities call to be embodied so that you are living them through life and bringing them to life as a marker of who you are.

Activations are the work to achieve in the moment; characteristics which, through consistent practice, support and empower you and also, with some Signatures, aid with enabling their qualities.

Soul Prompts are a key challenge to overcome or master, releasing limitations within your mind, emotional resonance or energy.

Qualities, activations and soul prompts **both** serve and support you **and** also limit you because energy requires balance and balance requires both positive and negative, black and white, yin and yang. Recognising where a quality limits you imparts valuable insight as the *limitation will also serve* something. In identifying this, you aid your ability to embody the quality more fully.

As an example: Devotion calls you to Integrity. This is empowering, it creates confidence and ensures authenticity and leading from principles which are rooted in probity. It limits you because integrity demands that you do the right thing, in the right way, for the right reason, which can sometimes be the harder path.

Self-awareness and self-reflection are always your superpowers with soul, so create time and space to spend with yourself in reflection and contemplation, fostering insight and specific understanding. A better quality question will always result in receiving a better quality answer.

If you want to take your work deeper, consider being asked to *master* your foundation Signature's qualities and activations and being asked *to step into* your leading Signature's qualities and activations.

Qualities

The Signature qualities are practical and relatable. They are attributes which will greatly benefit you and your (soul) purpose if you can align with and embody them through all aspects of being and life.

As you look at those relating to the Soul Signature you want to activate, think about:

- Where do you naturally align? What qualities do you meet with ease, and how does that support and empower you? Where do they limit you? Does that limitation serve you?
- How does not embodying a quality support you? Does it make life easier in the moment? Can you meet it and how would that serve you? Would embodying it also limit you?
- How can you live the qualities within life and, importantly, if you did, what benefit would that bring? The benefit will enable you to do the work!

For instance, with Initiation:

Do you think outside the box and do things differently or do you follow all the rules and conform? Where does conforming serve you? (e.g., perhaps it keeps you safe or creates a sense of belonging?) Where does it limit you? (e.g., does it prevent you from seeing opportunities to move forward or believing you can do things differently?)

If you could embody a greater level of innovation (in any area), how would that serve you? Would it also limit you? If so, how? What would meeting innovation require of you? Can you meet that and are you willing to?

For ease, the Signature qualities are listed below:

Initiation	Innovation, Direction, Curiosity
Resonance	Belief, Flow, Aligned Energy
Commitment	Truth, Discernment, Progress
Anchor	Reinvention, Growth, Creativity
Feminine	Courage, Intuition, Receptivity
Masculine	Strategy, Discipline, Structure
Emergence	Growth Mindset, Vision, Risk-taking
Surrender	Collaboration, Service, Purpose
Transformation	Balance, Freedom, Expansion
Integration	Resourcefulness, Clarity, Evolution
Devotion	Leadership, Mastery, Integrity

Activations

Most activations are traits you'll recognise and can relate to. Some Signatures do have more spiritually-based activations. Soul *always meets you where you are*, so with Unity Consciousness, for example (a Devotion Signature activation), <u>always</u> work with it in relation to what it means to you at *this moment in time*.

- Consider what activations are naturally present with you; do you utilise them fully? Could you activate them further? Can you see how they support you?
- Which activations do you *know* you either step back from or sabotage? Do you know why? Often this

can be about trust; the 'why' is where clearing and reframing need to happen.

- Which activation shows up consistently in life as an 'ask'?
- What is this trying to enable for you and how might that change life or change you? How does, or would, meeting an activation serve you? How would it limit you (or what responsibility would it place upon you)?

For example, with Commitment's Truth of Self, some of the questions you might ask yourself could be:

How honest are you (to yourself) about who you are? What shadow aspects do you not acknowledge? What light aspects don't you want to face? Where would these ask you to accept more or who would they ask you to become? How do these keep you safe (serving you)? How do they limit you? If you were *radically honest* in owning everything you are, *what would you have to accept or change*? Where does that liberate you? Where does it constrict you? How would you feel if you could not meet that acceptance or change?

Again, for ease, the activations are below:

Initiation	Adaptability, Resourcefulness, Trust
Resonance	Universal Awareness, New Possibilities
Commitment	Courageous Expression, Truth of Self, Clear Sight
Anchor	Universal Consciousness, Embracing Change, Creativity
Feminine	Empowered Intuition, Receptivity, Allowing
Masculine	Logical Action, Disciplined Approach
Emergence	Adventure, Growth, Passionate Direction
Surrender	Self-belief, Service, Unity
Transformation	Self-acceptance, Forgiveness, Universal Love
Integration	Liberation, Confidence, Present Moment Awareness
Devotion	Unity Consciousness, Divine Expression, Grace

Soul Prompts

Soul prompts are the consistent challenges you will recognise! Overcoming these creates a mental, emotional or energetic shift which supports you personally, within life generally or within business to embody the energy of that Soul Signature to a greater degree, allowing it to serve you more deeply.

Consider the soul prompt of your chosen Signature and ask yourself simply whether you do or don't meet it, what would enable you to meet it and whether you can. For example:

- (Transformation) Do you face fear through trust? (Masculine) Does your belief encourage success? If yes, fabulous! If not, think about:

- (Transformation) Can you face fear through trust? (Masculine) Could your belief encourage success? If yes, consciously be aware of actioning that at the next opportunity; if not, consider:
- What is stopping you? Do you know *why?* (Perceived fear, limiting belief or low self-worth, previous experience, for instance). How can you cultivate the ability you require to meet that soul prompt and move through it?
- If you did, what would this enable within you or your life? What difference would this make which would deeply support and serve you?
- Where would it limit you and how could you accept that and neutralise the limitation within your mind or emotions?

Here are the soul prompts for each Signature:

Initiation	Surrender Expectations and Allow
Resonance	Release Limiting Mindsets
Commitment	Detach from Judgement, Illusion and Fear
Anchor	Shed Who You No Longer Are
Feminine	Embrace Courage to Find Freedom
Masculine	Belief Encourages Success
Emergence	Courage Neutralises Self-Sabotage
Surrender	Accept Divine Purpose
Transformation	Face Fear Through Trust
Integration	Allow Change to be a Friend
Devotion	Embrace the Process of Life

Soul is a continuously expanding and evolving energy; it will always meet you where you are which means it will always meet you at varying levels within your awareness and growth. As with all aspects of self-development and self-reflective work, you can meet the same challenge at a different level as your awareness expands and you participate more deeply in your journey.

32

ACTIVATING A SIGNATURE FOR BUSINESS

ONE OF THE incredible benefits of working with Soul Signatures is the ability to use them to support your business; to align to a specific Signature because its qualities or activations will directly impress something which serves it.

Practically, you simply activate a Signature by *choosing to work* with its qualities, activations or soul prompt. As you consciously choose to work on embodying the vision for your business or working on enabling more of a growth mindset, you are activating Emergence. There will still be work to move through challenges or resistance, but Emergence will support that process.

If you know your business needs more structure, activate the Masculine Signature by creating a strategy or implementing processes. As you start work and the Signature activates, you will either feel more motivated, meet the work with greater ease, or you'll draw to you people, processes or systems which can support what you need to do.

If your business is very process-led and strategic and it needs to develop a more caring environment for you or your team, activate the Feminine Signature by creating space to receive yourself or your team's insight or ideas - an event, team building, a culture of openness and nurturing talent are all indicative of the Feminine Signature.

33

ENERGETIC ALIGNMENT TO SOUL SIGNATURES

The Signatures themselves are the energetic representation that you'll work with. They were shared with me as a visualised aspect of the energy matrix of soul which, as it naturally oscillates within our energy, triggers specific points of light that 'activate' respective Signatures within its' matrix, generating an energetic ripple within you which initiates a process of learning, growth, realisation etc.

As an energetic imprint, they work. The energy within the image interacts with your energy and a response is generated, sometimes immediately and at other times within a few days, as the Signature expands and settles, and its influence is received and accepted on an energetic level.

I would encourage you to work with the Signatures intuitively. You might have an instinctive knowing of what to do - if so, *please follow that urge* because you will be in direct communication with soul at that time! However, I have detailed three specific practices which I work with for clients, and that I use personally. These support the Signatures' activations or an awareness of what they are trying to support or enable with or within you.

I encourage you to be open and curious and to question rather than doubt. Questioning says, "I've had an experience, I am not sure what it was or what it means but I'm interested to know more." Doubting says, "I don't believe the experience which just occurred" - it is disempowering and can close both your energy and awareness down.

Note: It can be useful to have an awareness of grounding or centring techniques before undertaking any energetic or meditative work. This ensures that you are fully present and aligned as you go about your day afterwards. Grounding can be as simple as feeling your feet firmly on the floor, breathing through the body to feel it become slightly heavier - 'ground' - or having a glass of water. Centring is the ability to align yourself so that you feel calm, present and focused - this can be done by focusing on the breath. There is a wealth of information online if you are new to any aspect of meditative or energetic work.

Meditation

This is a meditative practice that you can use to enable a personal relationship to develop with a specific Signature over time, activating it but also cultivating a deeper understanding of its alignment, purpose and support with you and for you.

Make yourself comfortable - sit rather than lay, and give yourself some uninterrupted time. Focus on the Signature you are working with or drawn to; really see it and carry that with you as you close your eyes and move into a state of stillness. Allow your breathing to settle into a rhythm or use it as a focus to enable a state of stillness.

Allow time to feel into your space, to sense the body relaxing and your focus steadying into your stillness, so that you are more aware of your presence than distractions.

Hold the Signature in your awareness or your mind's eye and just allow it to be whatever it needs to be. You may lose the sense of its image and sense a light, a flow of energy or a colour, for example.

How do you feel as you sit with it? Are there words, insight or do emotions rise? Do they mean anything? Try not to attach to anything (energy is fluid); just acknowledge any experience and give thanks.

Gently bring awareness to your breath, focus on the seat you are sitting on, and feel your feet and fingers. When you are fully present, journal on anything that arose. If what arose was abstract, don't force meaning or understanding. The language of soul is not linear; meaning will emerge as your connection and communication progress.

You are in direct communication and connection with soul through the Soul Signature. Make time to practice regularly and both your personal awareness of soul itself, and your understanding of how the Signature is specifically working with you will develop.

Please refer to the Resources page for how to access a guided version of this practice.

Activating a Signature through Breath

This practice supports your intention to activate a specific Signature. *You are consciously choosing to give it permission to be more present and active within you.* There *will* be work which arises from this.

Make yourself comfortable - sit rather than lay, and give yourself some uninterrupted time. Focus on the visual representation of the Signature you want to activate. Really see it or feel it.

Relax as you focus on your breathing, and then gently, with each breath, visualise or imagine (energy follows intention so imagination enables energy) the Signature being drawn into your energy and physical body.

See it or feel it within you; allow your breath (intention) to move it down to your hara (the energetic centre, just below your belly button and in the centre of your abdomen). Each breath allows it to sink deeper. Take your time and allow the Signature to move through your energy and your body at its own pace.

Eventually, you will feel it 'expand' through the abdomen area (you may feel the expansion or you may simply know it); as it does this, it is activating. You will then feel it 'settle' - this may feel grounding, you may experience what appears to be a slight heaviness in your abdomen or you may be aware of the Signature just contracting slightly and 'fitting' into place.

As it settles, be open to any experience or awareness (there may be none or there may be some); stay in the stillness for a moment and then move your focus to the present moment, ground through feeling your feet firmly on the floor and allow yourself to centre.

The Signature has activated. If any insight arose or you experienced specific awareness, words or guidance through the process, jot them down. As the Signature's activation ripples through your energy, it will start to influence you - insight will rise or you may have an a-ha moment about something. Situations or circumstances may appear that cause a response to ask you to step into the qualities or activations of the Signature. You may also experience a desire to just do that and have a greater sense of assuredness that you can.

Please refer to the Resources page for how to access a guided version of this practice.

Using Signatures for Insight

This practice supports you in focusing your self-work in a specific area, based on your chakra system, your internal energetic system.

Chakras are vortexes of energy; central processors for every aspect of our being, taking in and distributing life force energy, releasing stagnant energies and supporting us to process life. Everything we think or feel can have an effect on our chakras. Tuning into their energy can lend intuitive wisdom to support us in determining behaviours, thoughts and emotions which do not serve, inhibit or restrain a sense of greater self and sovereignty.

This process works with the seven main chakra centres, aligned along the spine from the top of the head to your coccyx.

To start, find a quiet space and some time and focus on the visual representation of the Signature you're drawn to or are working with - see it or feel it as a living energy.

Allow yourself to relax and gently, with each breath, visualise or imagine the Signature being drawn into your energy and physical body.

As you see it, know it or feel it within you, allow yourself to relax further, breathing gently and rhythmically. Give the Signature permission to settle in your energy and be aware of where it does settle.

If it simply expands within your energy and settles in your hara (the intention in the previous practice), then the Signature is simply active and aligned within your energy and doesn't require a particular focus.

However, if the Signature settles in a chakra, then that chakra is where insight is required in relation to the Signature's qualities, activations or prompts.

Mentally note anything which arises during the process before bringing your focus to your breath, then to the present moment and allowing yourself to ground and centre.

I invite you now to move to some self-reflective work - reframing a limitation and aligning to the quality or activation is what the Signatures are all about and will provide a longer-term energetic balance than simply working on the chakra energy itself, although if you are an energy worker you can clear, align or balance the chakra as you are drawn to.

I've listed the primary chakra properties below but not in any depth - those of you who work energetically will know them anyway; those of you new to delving into energetics would benefit from information which offers a wider breadth than I am able to share here. I have suggested some natural synchronicities between the Signature/ chakra energy to help you identify what a specific Signature settling within a certain chakra might indicate. I've used the same two Signatures all the way through to give an idea of how the same

Signature responds within different chakras but these are simply suggestions. Use your reasoning, intuition and the qualities, activations and soul prompts to define the ask or limitation in relation to you - all the answers are in the Signature information in Part Two, in the chakra information below *and* in your own awareness.

Chakras, their properties and suggestions for Signature awareness

Crown Chakra

Connection to the Divine, Grounding Spirituality (into the body and into life), Recognition of a higher self or higher awareness, Service, Divine Purpose, Facilitation of communication/ connection with other aspects of energy (angels for example), Spiritual Achievement.

Feminine Signature resonance: Nurture your connection to a higher sense of self, e.g., for a clearer sense of purpose or service. Can you create space to receive all of yourself/ your awareness?

Emergence Signature resonance: You, your path and/or vision has met a significant growth stage and seeks to enable a greater purpose; personal growth has opened a different level in how you seek to serve. Be aware of insight, follow any intuitive guidance and be open to opportunity.

Third Eye/ Brow Chakra

Balancing intuition with logic, Discernment, Clear-sight (free from illusion or fantasy), Clairvoyance, Cognition and mental acuity, Intuitive reasoning and perception, Inspiration.

This is where we understand and interpret our psychic ability, although much of that originates through the Solar Plexus Chakra

Feminine Signature resonance: How can you enable a greater trust of, and allow a deepening of, your intuition? What would build trust in what you know (i.e., feel deeply within) to be true rather than wondering whether you are imagining it?

Emergence Signature resonance: Is your vision clear? Do you know what you want to achieve and why? Do you understand the growth it will ask of you and are you willing to do the mindset work to meet that? Is there something new coming into view - do you/can you trust that it is soul-led?

Throat Chakra

Communication (with others and within ourselves, including the ability to listen), Self-acceptance, Truth (understanding, allowing, expressing), Expression (the ability to clearly express and how, e.g., with compassion), Honesty and integrity.

Feminine Signature resonance: Where do you need to be aware of using more nurturing words to yourself (or others)? Where do you need to speak your truth with compassionate courage?

Emergence Signature resonance: Do you know what your current limitations are within yourself, where you are inhibiting growth? Do you understand *why* they are? Articulating them will help you own and understand them, enabling you to reframe, release or move past them into new potential.

Heart Chakra

The Bridge between the higher and lower chakras, Balance (in terms of viewing the world from a place of peace and centred connection), Compassion and love (for self and others), Boundaries, Empathy, Aspirations, Resilience (emotional and mental), Courage.

Feminine Signature resonance: Where do you need to allow yourself to receive love, compassion or care, or to be more supported within life? Check your boundaries are working and are respected. What emotions are you not allowing yourself to receive, understand, heal or accept? These are constricting your ability to fully open to yourself.

Emergence Signature resonance: Your path may call you to risk all of yourself in this next stage - do you have the courage of your convictions and vision and can you dedicate yourself to them? Do you trust yourself fully? What work do you need to do to support that?

Solar Plexus Chakra

Confidence (personal identity, what we show to the world), Ego (balance), Self-awareness, Personal Responsibility, Accountability, Self-belief, Self-sabotage, Personal or Professional Achievement.

This is also our primary psychic centre, where we connect with other people and the world on a psychic level although interpretation usually happens within the Third Eye Chakra

Feminine Signature resonance: Where do you need to be more confident in allowing your intuition to lead and in letting it be seen? Can you find the courage to lead from that, no matter in how small a way?

Emergence Signature resonance: Don't allow yourself to sabotage your current path, growth or success. Find a way to enable courage to neutralise the self-sabotaging pattern which is presenting or about to. Stand in your personal authority (which is not ego) with confidence in your self, vision and abilities.

Sacral Chakra

Joy, Passion (for life), Creativity and creative process, Sexuality (healthy, functioning, enjoyment), Confidence (in body and skin, in bringing ideas to life), Motivation.

Feminine Signature resonance: Your passion, or creativity, is the key to unleashing your deepest nature and allowing yourself fully.

Emergence Signature resonance: Passion is calling, opening new possibilities and potential - are you ready for a new adventure? Can you find what you need to bring your passion and vision to life?

Base/ Root Chakra

Grounding, Security, safety and stability (in ourselves, in life and the world), Manifestation, Ability to generate financial stability/ security, Trust (in oneself and the process of life and in your ability to meet life), Vitality and drive.

Feminine Signature resonance: Nurture your physical body, it supports your vitality which supports everything else. How can you create space to trust in your ability to create stability and security for yourself?

Emergence Signature resonance: Your vision may be limited by your belief in your ability to generate financial stability or by a desire for security. How can you reframe this? Is your physical vitality affecting motivation or drive and the ability to meet the needs of your path or vision?

Activating a Signature with Crystals

This is a great process to use in addition to the other energetic processes to enhance the activation or to use instead of them. This is ideal if you'd rather work without meditation or drawing a Signature into your energy, especially if you are not confident with a visual/ meditative process, would rather ease into energy work if you are new to it, or would like a more practical energetic way to activate a Signature.

Ideally, I would suggest using clear quartz crystals as clear quartz amplifies, thereby enhancing the Signature resonance and activating it. Crystals don't need to be big, tumblestones or small points are perfect. Tumbles radiate energy whilst points direct it and so with points, you'll have a stronger activation (but please bear in mind that strong is not necessarily always best and you will have to meet that energy in the Signature's ask) whilst tumblestones generate (activate the Signature) as they radiate, taking slightly longer to fulfil the remit.

Place crystals on the activations points (as per the diagram for the Feminine Signature below) and leave the image and crystals somewhere they won't be disturbed. If using points, place the crystals with their points facing outward; even with central activation points, still ensure the crystal points face

outwards. Pointing outward expands the energy which activates the Signature.

Place crystals on the activation points

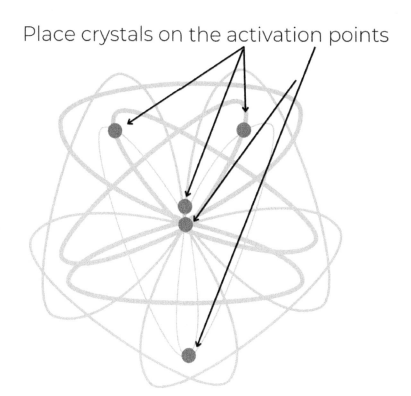

Leave them in place until you start to be aware of the Signature's influence and then remove them.

The intention is always relevant with crystals so as you place
them on the Signature, do so with the intention that you
would like to activate it. Trust that it will activate and
respond in a way which supports what you need.

Please do use the same crystal throughut rather than a variety of different ones; also, use *either* points *or* tumbles and not a mixture of both.

Please refer to the Resources page for how to access further information on using crystals to activate a Signature.

34

THE POWER OF YOUR FIRST NAME

BEFORE WE CLOSE THIS SECTION, I wanted to share the power of your full first name. Some of you will naturally use it, own it and its Signature will be impressive within your energy.

Some people don't like, and therefore don't use, their first name or only use an abbreviation; it can often be associated with childhood memories of your parents using it when scolding you!

Yet, your first name is a powerful personal energy. Owning it will liberate you from constraints or limitations linked with its use and it has the power to help you connect more fully with your soul energy as it is a potently personal part of your energetic matrix. Whilst it is a name you were given, rather than a name you yourself chose, it formed an (unconscious) part of your identity as an infant and child and so its energy is inherently significant. There are no coincidences so the name you were gifted offers a gift.

If you don't currently use your first name - or your first name in its full form - and when you think about using it, you tense up or your energy contracts, then it is energetically impacting you in a way that limits, and you will benefit by aligning your energy to your name and bringing it to a sense of balance within you.

You will have already identified its Signature through Part One, so use it. Look at the Signature and be aware of how you feel or what is alive in you as you look at the Signature. Do its qualities, activations or soul prompt resonate? It may be that you already have that Signature active in your profile, in which case play with your name. Roll it around your mouth. How does it really feel? What does it mean to you? When you say it, how does it sound and do you hear yourself saying it, or someone else?

Whilst this book isn't about working with your name or any other aspect of soul from a therapeutic perspective, having disowned my name of Nicola for most of my life, I can say with profound sincerity that owning it changed me: I stepped more fully into who I was, who I was born to be and that influenced who I allowed myself to grow into.

If we believe that soul is the divine essence that breathes into life within us as we first take breath, then everything leading into that moment is divinely guided by a power which orchestrates majesty and sets us upon a path with particular tools (name, date of birth, for example) for a specific purpose: being everything we can by being ourselves, fully.

Your name is part of that.

Note: If you have a middle name which you don't use and its Signature qualities can directly support or benefit you, you can activate it simply by starting to use that name - even if it is only to yourself - perhaps saying "good morning Jane Anne" when you are cleaning your teeth!

"Within every aspect of soul comes a moment which radiates confidence in everything you are"

That is Being Soul Confident

35

THE TWELFTH SIGNATURE

WE ALL HAVE the potential to master all of the qualities, activations and soul prompts of all the Soul Signatures. Some are always more naturally within our gift but all are present and all are possible.

What we need to do is work with conscious intent to master and embody, and to be consciously aware of where we step forward and where we step back.

As Soul Signatures naturally activate, they guide you to certain possibilities, opportunities and potential, yet you have to choose to embrace those possibilities, step into the opportunities and reach for the potential.

As with any other area of life where you wish to learn, develop, grow or excel, you have to do the work and, as you will have realised through your life, it is actually in the work itself that we find the enrichment we often associate with the goal - fulfilment, joy, wonder, purpose and meaning are just a few.

So... master the work and know that it is the path, that it is the spark which ignites everything else.

As you've moved through this book and worked out your Signatures, you may have noticed that Initiation and Resonance only rarely occur naturally, although they are always subconsciously present within, respectively, Integration and Devotion. As we reach the end of a cycle within any area of life and at any level or stage of development and evolution, the next potential has already begun weaving into existence.

Whilst all of the Signatures' qualities serve, support, empower, authorise and permit, Initiation and Resonance are of particular significance collectively - the ability to be curious about ourselves and life, to be open to doing things differently, to create new ways of being emotionally, intellectually, culturally has the potential to enable a more loving and inclusive space within this world for the next generations.

If we can open our minds and our hearts to the awareness of the energy which is inherent within all of us, is threaded through and around our world and our universe, and if we can hold the belief that all of that divinity is possible within a physical life, we will enable new possibilities which honour the connectedness within all things, and which serve this great planet who gives us life.

Therefore Initiation and Resonance are Signatures that have a collective and divine directive to impact and influence all of us for the greater good of humanity. However, where they do align within your personal profile their qualities have a personal influence and they can also be activated, as with any Signature, if you feel drawn to work with their qualities, activations or soul prompts.

Within all things, there are myriad endings and yet the beginnings of everything are always within our possibility - it is where hope lies and where we find a faith which renews with each sunrise. If we can align with our divine awareness and recognise the power of that through everything we are and everything we do, miracles can abound and you'll start to recognise yourself as the twelfth Signature - soul in perfect motion.

At the heart of your journey. Leading with soul, leading from soul and being soul confident by simply being fully, freely, wonderfully, consciously, divinely you.

RESOURCES

I'm delighted to be able to offer some resources to support you in working with and activating Soul Signatures.

You'll find the guided versions of the Meditation and Activating a Signature Through Breath practices detailed in Part Four of this book at:

https://nicolatonsager.co.uk/**being-soul-confident**/

I've also shared further information on Activating a Signature with Crystals if you'd like to take that a little bit deeper.

ACKNOWLEDGEMENTS

First of all, no journey is walked alone: to everyone who has supported me through all of my work over the years, through all of my learning and development, my deepest thank you.

To Shirley O'Donoghue – Shirley, without you guiding my first tentative steps into energy, Soul Signatures would not be here. Thank you for everything you do.

To Charlotte Carter for all of your immense encouragement to step into my limitless self and for your constant belief – thank you, thank you.

To Abigail Horne and everyone at Authors & Co for guiding me through publishing Being Soul Confident – you are amazing and I thank you so much for your commitment and inspiration. You are the dream makers!

For everyone who took a leap of faith in working with Soul Signatures with me as they found their light, their shape and started to come into being – *you* made this happen. Thank you.

Finally, to my mum, my most constant support who is always there for me, no matter what. I love you.

ABOUT THE AUTHOR

Nicola Tonsager is a spiritual and soul mentor, working with people who want that deep, soul connection; who feel disconnected from who they are – either through life, situations or the roles they play – and who want to reconnect with confidence, clarity and purpose. She also works with business owners who want to understand the inherent soul energy supporting their business.

With a twenty-five year background in energy and holistic practices, Nicola has taught to practitioner level in a range of therapies, run retreats and mentorships and has her own range of vibrational essences.

As a sensitive intuitive, she has had an awareness of energy since childhood but didn't realise what it was until she had her first direct experience of soul, a catalyst for learning all she could about the inherent energy that we are, and the wider energetic world which we are a part of.

Nicola believes passionately that we all matter, that what we do and how we do it makes a difference, and that it all starts with you being at the heart of your journey, inhabiting yourself fully with joy and purpose, being soul confident and living that in everything you do.

Nicola is a Foundation Activation of Transformation and a Leading Activation of Commitment. She knows the power and progress that is found by standing in one's own truth, certain in a sense of self, belief and trust. With Transformation, it took her until her early forties to find a balanced, consistent approach to change that created transformation and which she was then able to develop with her clients. Standing in her truth has always sustained her; the ability to lead from it has directly enabled her work with soul and the Soul Signatures.

Nicola offers group programmes and tailored one-to-one mentoring.

You can find Nicola online at the following links:

www.nicolatonsager.co.uk

instagram.com/nicolatonsager

Printed in Great Britain
by Amazon

21990744R00131